CAMBRIDGE LIBRARY COLLECTION

Books of enduring scholarly value

Printing and Publishing History

The interface between authors and their readers is a fascinating subject in its own right, revealing a great deal about social attitudes, technological progress, aesthetic values, fashionable interests, political positions, economic constraints, and individual personalities. This part of the Cambridge Library Collection reissues classic studies in the area of printing and publishing history that shed light on developments in typography and book design, printing and binding, the rise and fall of publishing houses and periodicals, and the roles of authors and illustrators. It documents the ebb and flow of the book trade supplying a wide range of customers with products from almanacs to novels, bibles to erotica, and poetry to statistics.

How to Form a Library

Henry Benjamin Wheatley (1838-1917) was a prolific writer on bibliography, literature and the arts. As founder of the Index Society, and editor of *The Bibliographer*, he was also involved in the foundation of the Library Association. In that context he wrote several works on library topics. *How to Form a Library* was published in 1886, when libraries where spreading rapidly throughout England. The book provides advice on the selection of material for different kinds of libraries and audiences, and suggests a list of core works. Although the choices reflect the period in which it was written – a point Wheatley makes about earlier lists – it nonetheless has a value in giving insight into the intellectual interests of the day. He was firmly against librarians acting as moral censors, and although his list of required reading is unlikely to be followed today, the book contains much valuable information on library history.

T0381703

How to Form a Library

Henry Benjamin Wheatley

CAMBRIDGE UNIVERSITY PRESS

Cambridge, New York, Melbourne, Madrid, Cape Town, Singapore,
São Paolo, Delhi, Dubai, Tokyo, Mexico City

Published in the United States of America by Cambridge University Press, New York

www.cambridge.org
Information on this title: www.cambridge.org/9781108021494

© in this compilation Cambridge University Press 2010

This edition first published 1886
This digitally printed version 2010

ISBN 978-1-108-02149-4 Paperback

The Book-Lover's Library.

Edited by

Henry B. Wheatley, F.S.A.

HOW
TO FORM A LIBRARY

BY

H. B. WHEATLEY, F.S.A.

LONDON
ELLIOT STOCK, 62 PATERNOSTER ROW
1886

PREFACE.

T will be generally allowed that a handy guide to the formation of libraries is required, but it may be that the difficulty of doing justice to so large a subject has prevented those who felt the want from attempting to fill it. I hope therefore that it will not be considered that I have shown temerity by stepping into the vacant place. I cannot hope to have done full justice to so important a theme in the small space at my disposal, but I think I can say that this little volume contains much information which the librarian and the book lover require and cannot easily obtain *elsewhere. They are probably acquainted with most of this information, but the memory will fail us at times and it is then convenient to have a record at hand.*

A book of this character is peculiarly open to criticism, but I hope the critics will give me credit for knowing more than I have set down. In making a list of books of reference, I have had to make a selection, and works have been before me that I have decided to omit, although some would think them as important as many of those I have included.

I need not extend this preface with any lengthy explanation of the objects of the book, as these are stated in the Introduction, but before concluding I may perhaps be allowed to allude to one personal circumstance. I had hoped to dedicate this first volume of the Book Lover's

Library to HENRY BRADSHAW, *one of the most original and most learned biblio-graphers that ever lived, but before it was finished the spirit of that great man had passed away to the inexpressible grief of all who knew him. It is with no desire to shield myself under the shelter of a great name, but with a reverent wish to express my own sense of our irreparable loss that I dedicate this book (though all unworthy of the honour) to his memory.*

HOW TO FORM A LIBRARY.

INTRODUCTION.

ALTHOUGH there can be little
difference of opinion among book
lovers as to the need of a Handbook which shall answer satisfactorily the
question—"How to Form a Library"—it
does not follow that there will be a like
agreement as to the best shape in which to
put the answer. On the one side a string
of generalities can be of no use to any one,
and on the other a too great particularity
of instruction may be resented by those who
only require hints on a few points, and feel
that they know their own business better
than any author can tell them.

One of the most important attempts to
direct the would-be founder of a Library

in his way was made as long ago as 1824
by Dr. Dibdin, and the result was entitled
The Library Companion.[1] The book could
never have been a safe guide, and now it is
hopelessly out of date. Tastes change, and
many books upon the necessity of possessing
which Dibdin enlarges are now little valued.
Dr. Hill Burton writes of this book as follows
in his *Book-Hunter:* "This, it will be observed, is not intended as a manual of rare
or curious, or in any way peculiar books,
but as the instruction of a Nestor on the best
books for study and use in all departments
of literature. Yet one will look in vain
there for such names as Montaigue, Shaftes-
bury, Benjamin Franklin, D'Alembert, Tur-
got, Adam Smith, Malebranche, Lessing,
Goethe, Schiller, Fénélon, Burke, Kant,
Richter, Spinoza, Flechier, and many
others. Characteristically enough, if you
turn up Rousseau in the index, you will find
Jean Baptiste, but not Jean Jacques. You

---

[1] " *The Library Companion, or the Young Man's
Guide and the Old Man's Comfort in the Choice of
a Library.* By the Rev. T. F. Dibdin, F.R.S., A.S.,
London, 1824."

will search in vain for Dr. Thomas Reid
the metaphysician, but will readily find
Isaac Reed the editor. If you look for
Molinæus, or Du Moulin, it is not there,
but alphabetical vicinity gives you the good
fortune to become acquainted with "Moule,
Mr., his *Bibliotheca Heraldica*." The name
of Hooker will be found, not to guide the
reader to the *Ecclesiastical Polity*, but to
Dr. Jackson Hooker's *Tour in Iceland*.
Lastly, if any one shall search for Hartley
on Man, he will find in the place it might
occupy, or has reference to, the editorial
services of ' Hazlewood, Mr. Joseph.' "

Although this criticism is to a great extent true, it does not do justice to Dibdin's
book, which contains much interesting and
valuable matter, for if the *Library Companion*
is used not as a Guide to be followed, but
as a book for reference, it will be found of
considerable use.

William Goodhugh's *English Gentleman's
Library Manual, or a Guide to the Formation of a Library of Select Literature*, was
published in 1827. It contains classified

lists of library books, but these are not now of much value, except for the notes which accompany the titles, and make this work eminently readable. There are some literary anecdotes not to be found elsewhere.

A most valuable work of reference is Mr. Edward Edwards's Report on the formation of the Manchester Free Library, which was printed in 1851. It is entitled, "*Librarian's First Report to the Books Sub-Committee on the Formation of the Library, June* 30, 1851, *with Lists of Books suggested for purchase.*"   The Lists are arranged in the following order:—

1. Works—collective and miscellaneous —of Standard British authors; with a selection of those of the Standard authors of America.
2. Works relative to the History, Topography, and Biography of the United Kingdom, and of the United States of America.
3. Works relative to Political Economy, Finance, Trade, Commerce, Agriculture, Mining, Manufactures, Inland Communication, and Public Works.

4. Works relating to Physics, Mathematics, Mechanics, Practical Engineering, Arts, and Trades, etc.
5. Voyages and Travels.
6. Works on Zoology, Botany, Mineralogy, and Geology.
7. Periodical Publications and Transactions of Learned Societies (not included in Lists 2, 3, or 6), Collections, Encyclopædias, Gazetteers, Atlases, Dictionaries, Bibliographies, Indexes, etc.

These draft lists include 4582 distinct works, extending to about 12,438 volumes, including pamphlets, but exclusive of 553 Parliamentary Papers and Reports, or *Blue Books.* Such a practically useful collection of lists of books will not easily be found elsewhere.

Mr. Edwards gives some rules for the formation of Libraries in the second volume of his *Memoirs of Libraries* (p. 629), where he writes, " No task is more likely to strip a man of self-conceit than that of having to frame, and to carry out in detail a plan for the formation of a large Library. When he has once got beyond those departments of knowledge in which his own pursuits and tastes have specially interested him, the duty becomes a difficult one, and the certainty, that with his best efforts, it will be very imperfectly performed is embarrassing and painful. If, on the other hand, the task be imposed upon a 'Committee,' there ensues almost the certainty that its execution will depend at least as much on chance as on plan : that responsibility will be so attenuated as to pass off in vapour; and that the collection so brought together will consist of parts bearing but a chaotic sort of relation to the whole."

Mr. Henry Stevens printed in 1853 his pretty little book entitled *Catalogue of my English Library*, which contains a very useful selection of Standard books. In his Introduction the author writes, "It was my intention in the outset not to exceed 4000 volumes, but little by little the list has increased to 5751 volumes. I have been considerably puzzled to know what titles

to strike out in my next impression, being
well aware that what is trash to one person
is by no means such to another; also that
many books of more merit than those admitted have been omitted. You may not
think it difficult to strike out twenty authors,
and to add twenty better ones in their place,
but let me relate to you a parable. I re-
quested twenty men, whose opinions on the
Literary Exchange are as good as those
of the Barings or the Rothschilds on the
Royal, each to expunge twenty authors and
to insert twenty others of better standing
in their places, promising to exclude in my
next impression any author who should
receive more than five votes. The result
was, as may be supposed, not a single ex-
pulsion or addition."

In 1855 Mons. Hector Bossange produced a companion volume, entitled *Ma
Bibliothèque Française.* It contains a select
list of about 7000 volumes, and is completed with Indexes of Subjects, Authors,
and Persons.

For helpful Bibliographical Guides we

often have to look to the United States,
and we do not look in vain. A most useful Handbook, entitled *The Best Reading*,
was published in 1872 by George P. Putman,
and the work edited by F. B. Perkins is
now in its fourth edition.[1] The books are
arranged in an alphabet of subjects, and the
titles are short, usually being well within a
single line. A very useful system of appraise-
ment of the value of the books is adopted.
Thus: *a*, means that the book so marked is
considered *the* book, or as good as any, *at a
moderate cost;* *b* means, in like manner, the
best of the more elaborate or costly books
on the subject.   In the department of
FICTION, a more precise classification has
been attempted, in which a general idea

[1] *The Best Reading* : Hints on the Selection of
Books ; on the Formation of Libraries, Public and
Private ; on Courses of Reading, etc., with a Classified
Bibliography for every reference.   Fourth revised and
enlarged edition, continued to August, 1876, with the
addition of Select Lists of the best French, German,
Spanish, and Italian Literature.   Edited by Frederic
Beecher Perkins ; New York, G. P. Putnam's Sons,
1881.   Second Series, 1876 to 1882, by Lynds E.
Jones.

of the relative importance of the *authors* is indicated by the use of the letters *a*, *b*, and *c*, and of the relative value of their several works by the asterisks * and **."

Having noted a few of the Guides which are now at hand for the use of the founders of a library, we may be allowed to go back somewhat in time, and consider how our predecessors treated this same subject, and we can then conclude the present Introduction with a consideration of the less ambitious attempts to instruct the book collector which may be found in papers and articles.

One of the earliest works on the formation of a library was written by Bishop Cardona, and published at Tarragona in 1587, in a thin volume entitled *De regia S. Laurentii Bibliothecâ. De Pontificia Vaticana* [etc.].

Justus Lipsius wrote his *De Bibliothecis Syntagma* at the end of the sixteenth century, and next in importance we come to Gabriel Naudé, who published one of the most famous of bibliographical essays.

The first edition was published at Paris in 1627, and the second edition in 1644. This was reprinted in Paris by J. Liseux in 1876— "*Advis pour dresser une Bibliothèque, presenté à Monseigneur le President de Mesme,* par G. Naudé P.   Paris, chez François Farga, 1627."

This essay was translated by John Evelyn, and dedicated to Lord Chancellor Clarendon. "*Instructions concerning erecting of a Library ;* Presented to My Lord the President De Mesme.   By Gabriel Naudeus P., and now interpreted by Jo. Evelyn, Esquire, London, 1661."

Naudé enlarges on the value of Catalogues, and recommends the book-buyer to make known his desires, so that others may help him in the search, or supply his wants.   He specially mentions two modes of forming a library ; one is to buy libraries entire, and the other is to hunt at book-stalls.   He advised the book-buyer not to spend too much upon bindings.

Naudé appears to have been a born librarian, for at the early age of twenty

the President De Mesme appointed him to
take charge of his library. He left his em-
ployer in 1626, in order to finish his medical
studies. Cardinal Bagni took him to Rome,
and when Bagni died, Naudé became librarian
to Cardinal Barberini. Richelieu recalled
him to Paris in 1642, to act as his librarian,
but the Minister dying soon afterwards,
Naudé took the same office under Mazarin.
During the troubles of the Fronde, the
librarian had the mortification of seeing the
library which he had collected dispersed;
and in consequence he accepted the offer
of Queen Christina, to become her librarian
at Stockholm. Naudé was not happy abroad,
and when Mazarin appealed to him to
reform his scattered library, he returned
at once, but died on the journey home at
Abbeville, July 29, 1653.

The Mazarin Library consisted of more
than 40,000 volumes, arranged in seven
rooms filled from top to bottom. It was
rich in all classes, but more particularly in
Law and Physic. Naudé described it with
enthusiasm as "the most beautiful and best

furnished of any library now in the world, or that is likely (if affection does not much deceive me) ever to be hereafter." Such should be a library in the formation of which the Kings and Princes and Ambassadors of Europe were all helpers. Naudé in another place called it "the work of my hands and the miracle of my life." Great therefore was his dejection when the library was dispersed. Of this he said, "Beleeve, if you please, that the ruine of this Library will be more carefully marked in all Histories and Calendars, than the taking and sacking of Constantinople." Naudé's letter on the destruction of the Mazarin Library was published in London in 1652, and the pamphlet was reprinted in the *Harleian Miscellany*. "*News from France, or a Description of the Library of Cardinall Mazarini, before it was utterly ruined*. Sent in a letter from G. Naudæus, Keeper of the Publick Library. London, Printed for Timothy Garthwait, 1652." 4to. 4 leaves.

In 1650 was published at London, by

Samuel Hartlib, a little book entitled, "*The Reformed Librarie Keeper, with a Supplement to the Reformed School, as Subordinate to Colleges in Universities.* By John Durie. London, William Du-Gard, 1650."[1]

John Durie's ideas on the educational value of Libraries and the high function of the Librarian are similar to those enunciated by Carlyle, when he wrote, "The true University of these days is a Collection of Books." Of this point, as elaborated in the proposal to establish Professorships of Bibliography, we shall have something more to say further on.

It is always interesting to see the views of great men exemplified in the selection of books for a Library, and we may with advantage study the lists prepared by George III. and Dr. Johnson. The King was a collector of the first rank, as is evidenced by his fine library, now in the British

[1] Dr. Richard Garnett read an interesting paper on this book under the title of *Librarianship in the Seventeenth Century*, before the Library Association. See *Library Chronicle*, vol. i. p. 1 (1884).

Museum, and he knew his books well.
When he was about to visit Weymouth, he
wrote to his bookseller for the following
books to be supplied to him to form a closet
library at that watering place.   The list was
written from memory, and it was printed by
Dibdin in his *Library Companion*, from the
original document in the King's own handwriting :

> The Holy Bible. 2 vols. 8vo. Cambridge.
> New Whole Duty of Man.   8vo.
> The Annual Register.   25 vols.   8vo.
> The History of England, by Rapin.   21
>   vols.   8vo.   1757.
> Elémens de l'Histoire de France, par
>   Millot.   3 vols.   12mo.   1770.
> Siècle de Louis XIV., par Voltaire. 12mo.
> Siècle de Louis XV., par Voltaire. 12mo.
> Commentaries on the Laws of England,
>   by Sir William Blackstone.   4 vols.
>   8vo.   Newest Edition.
> The Justice of the Peace and Parish
>   Officer, by R. Burn.   4 vols.   8vo.
> An Abridgement of Samuel Johnson's
>   Dictionary.   2 vols.   8vo.

Dictionnaire François et Anglois, par
  M. A. Boyer. 8vo.
The Works of the English Poets, by Sam.
  Johnson. 68 vols. 12mo.
A Collection of Poems, by Dodsley, Pearch,
  and Mendez. 11 vols. 12mo.
A Select Collection of Poems, by J.
  Nichols. 8 vols. 12mo.
Shakespeare's Plays, by Steevens.
Œuvres de Destouches. 5 vols. 12mo.
The Works of Sir William Temple. 4
  vols. 8vo.
The Works of Jonathan Swift. 24 vols.
  12mo.
Dr. Johnson recommended the following
list of books to the Rev. Mr. Astle, of Ash-
bourne, Derbyshire, as a good working
collection : —
  Rollin's Ancient History.
  Universal History (Ancient).
  Puffendorf's Introduction to History.
  Vertot's History of the Knights of Malta.
  Vertot's Revolutions of Portugal.
  Vertot's Revolutions of Sweden.
  Carte's History of England.

Present State of England.
Geographical Grammar.
Prideaux's Connection.
Nelson's Feasts and Fasts.
Duty of Man.
Gentleman's Religion.
Clarendon's History.
Watts's Improvement of the Mind.
Watts's Logick.
Nature Displayed.
Lowth's English Grammar.
Blackwall on the Classicks.
Sherlock's Sermons.
Burnet's Life of Hale.
Dupin's History of the Church.
Shuckford's Connection.
Law's Serious Call.
Walton's Complete Angler.
Sandys's Travels.
Sprat's History of the Royal Society.
England's Gazetteer.
Goldsmith's Roman History.
Some Commentaries on the Bible.

It is curious to notice in both these lists how many of the books are now quite superseded.

In another place Boswell tells us what were Johnson's views on book collecting. "When I mentioned that I had seen in the King's Library sixty-three editions of my favourite *Thomas à Kempis*, amongst which it was in eight languages, Latin, German, French, Italian, Spanish, English, Arabick, and Armenian, he said he thought it unnecessary to collect many editions of a book, which were all the same, except as to the paper and print; he would have the original, and all the translations, and all the editions which had any variations in the text. He approved of the famous collection of editions of Horace by Douglas, mentioned by Pope, who is said to have had a closet filled with them; and he said every man should try to collect one book in that manner, and present it to a Publick Library."

Dr. Johnson's notion as to the collection of editions which are alike except in the point of paper is scarcely sound, but it has been held by a librarian of the present day, as I know to my cost. On one occasion I was anxious to see several copies of the

2

first folio of Shakespeare (1623), and I visited a certain library which possessed more than one. The librarian expressed the opinion that one was quite sufficient for me to see, as "they were all alike."

The possessor of a Private Library can act as a *censor morum* and keep out of his collection any books which offend against good morals, but this *role* is one which is unfit for the librarian of a Public Library. He may put difficulties in the way of the ordinary reader seeing such books, but nevertheless they should be in his library for the use of the student. A most amusing instance of misapplied zeal occurred at the Advocates' Library on the 27th June, 1754. The Minutes tell the tale in a way that speaks for itself and requires no comment. "Mr. James Burnet [afterwards Lord Monboddo], and Sir David Dalrymple [afterwards Lord Hailes], Curators of the Library, having gone through some accounts of books lately bought, and finding therein the three following French books: *Les Contes de La Fontaine, L'Histoire Amoureuse des Gaules* and *L'Ecumoire,* they ordain that the said books be struck out of the Catalogue of the Library, and removed from the shelves, as indecent books, unworthy of a place in a learned Library."

At a Conference of Representatives of Institutions in Union with the Society of Arts held in July, 1885, the question of the compilation of a Catalogue of Books fitted for the Libraries of Institutions was raised, and shortly afterwards was published, under the sanction of the Council, "*A Handbook of Mechanics' Institutions, with Priced Catalogue of Books suitable for Libraries, and Periodicals for Reading Rooms,* by W. H. J. Traice." A second edition of this book was published in 1863. The list, however, is not now of much use, as many of the books have been superseded. Theology and Politics are not included in the classification.

In 1868 Mr. Mullins read a paper before a Meeting of the Social Science Association at Birmingham, on the management of Free Libraries, and, in its reprinted form, this has become a Handbook on the subject: "*Free Libraries and News-rooms, their Formation*

and Management. By J. D. Mullins, Chief
Librarian, Birmingham Free Libraries.
Third edition. London, Sotheran and Co.,
1879." An appendix contains copies of the
Free Libraries Acts and Amendments, and
a " Short List of Books for a Free Lending
Library, ranging in price from 1*s.* to 7*s.* 6*d.*
per volume."

Mr. Axon read a paper on the Formation
of Small Libraries intended for the Co-
Operative Congress in 1869, which was
reprinted as a pamphlet of eight pages :
*"Hints on the Formation of Small Libraries
intended for Public Use.* By Wm. E. A. Axon.
London, N. Trübner and Co."

Mr. A. R. Spofford has given a valuable
list of books and articles in periodicals,
on the subject of Libraries in chapter 36
(Library Bibliography), of the *Report on
Public Libraries in the U.S.* (1876).

The volume of *Transactions and Proceed-
ings of the Conference of Librarians,* London,
1877, contains two papers on the Selection
of Books, one by Mr. Robert Harrison,
Librarian of the London Library, and the

other by the late Mr. James M. Anderson, Assistant Librarian of the University of St. Andrews. Mr. Harrison gives the following as the three guiding principles of selection in forming a library: 1. Policy; 2. Utility; 3. Special or Local Appropriateness; and he deals with each successively. Mr. Anderson writes that "the selection of books should invariably be made (1) in relation to the library itself, and (2) in relation to those using it."

We have chiefly to do with the formation of libraries, and therefore the use made of them when they are formed cannot well be enlarged upon here, but a passing note may be made on the proposal which has been much discussed of late years, viz. that for Professorships of Books and Reading. The United States Report on Public Libraries contains a chapter on this subject by F. B. Perkins and William Matthews (pp. 230–251), and Mr. Axon also contributed a paper at the First Annual Meeting of the Library Association. The value of such chairs, if well filled, is self-evident, for it takes a man a long time (without teaching) to learn how best to use books, but very special men would be required as Professors. America has done much to show what the duties of such a Professor should be, and Harvard College is specially fortunate in possessing an officer in Mr. Justin Winsor who is both a model librarian and a practical teacher of the art of how best to use the books under his charge.

CHAPTER I.

How Men have Formed Libraries.

S long as books have existed there have been book collectors. It is easy now to collect, for books of interest are to be found on all sides; but in old times this was not so, and we must therefore admire the more those men who formed their libraries under the greatest difficulties. In a book devoted to the formation of libraries it seems but fair to devote some space to doing honour to those who have formed libraries, and perhaps some practical lessons may be learned from a few historical facts.

Englishmen may well be proud of Richard Aungerville de Bury, a man occupying a busy and exalted station, who not only collected books with ardour united with

judgment, but has left for the benefit of
later ages a manual which specially endears
his memory to all book lovers.

He collected books, and often took them
in place of corn for tithes and dues, but he
also produced books, for he kept copyists
in his house. Many of these books were
carefully preserved in his palace at Durham,
but it is also pleasant to think of some of
them being carefully preserved in the noble
mansion belonging to his see which stood
by the side of the Thames, and on the site
of the present Adelphi.

Petrarch was a book-loving poet, and he
is said to have met the book-loving eccle-
siastic Richard de Bury at Rome. He gave
his library to the Church of St. Mark at
Venice in 1362 ; but the guardians allowed
the books to decay, and few were rescued.
Boccaccio bequeathed his library to the
Augustinians at Florence, but one cannot
imagine the books of the accomplished
author of the *Decameron* as very well suited
for the needs of a religious society, and it
was probably weeded before Boccaccio's

death. The remains of the library are still shown to visitors in the Laurentian Library, the famous building due to the genius of Michael Angelo.

Cardinal John Bessarion gave his fine collection (which included about 600 Greek MSS.) to St. Mark's in 1468, and in the letter to the Doge which accompanied his gift, he tells some interesting particulars of his early life as a collector. He writes, " From my youth I have bestowed my pains and exertion in the collection of books on various sciences. In former days I copied many with my own hands, and I have employed on the purchase of others such small means as a frugal and thrifty life permitted me to devote to the purpose."

The Rev. Joseph Hunter printed in 1831 a valuable Catalogue of the Library of the Priory of Bretton in Yorkshire, and added to it some notices of the Libraries belonging to other Religious Houses, in which he gives us a good idea of the contents of these libraries. He writes, "On comparing the Bretton Catalogue with that of other

religious communities, we find the libraries
of the English monasteries composed of
very similar materials. They consisted of—

1. The Scriptures; and these always in
   an English or the Latin version. A
   Greek or Hebrew Manuscript of the
   Scriptures is not found in Leland's
   notes, or, I believe, in any of the
   catalogues. In Wetstein's Catalogue
   of MSS. of the New Testament, only
   one (Codex 59) is traced into the
   hands of an English community of
   religious.
2. The Commentators.
3. The Fathers.
4. Services and Rituals of the Church.
5. Writers in the Theological Contro-
   versies of the Middle Ages.
6. Moral and Devotional Writings.
7. Canon Law.
8. The Schoolmen.
9. Grammatical Writers.
10. Writers in Mathematics and Physics.
11. Medical Writers.
12. Collections of Epistles.

13. The Middle Age Poets and Romance-
     Writers.
14. The Latin Classics.
15. The Chronicles.
16. The Historical Writings of doubtful
     authority, commonly called Legends.
Most of the manuscripts which composed
the monastic libraries were destroyed at
the Reformation."

Humphry Plantagenet Duke of Gloucester,
whose fame has been so lasting as the 'good
Duke Humphry,' was also a book-collector
of renown ; but most of the old libraries
we read about have left but little record of
their existence : thus the Common Library
at Guildhall, founded by Dick Whittington
in 1420, and added to by John Carpenter,
the Town Clerk of London, has been entirely destroyed, the books having, in the
first instance, been carried away by Edward
Seymour Duke of Somerset.

Although, as we have seen from Mr.
Hunter's remarks, there was a considerable amount of variety in the subjects
of these manuscript collections, we must

still bear in mind that in a large number
of instances the contents of the libraries
consisted of little more than Breviaries and
Service Books.   It has been pointed out
that this fact is illustrated by the union of
the offices of Precentor and Armarius in
one person, who had charge of the Library
(Armarium) and its great feeder, the Writing-
room (Scriptorium), as well as the duty of
leading the singing in the church.   Many
lists of old libraries have been preserved,
and these have been printed in various
bibliographical works, thus giving us a
valuable insight into the reading of our
forefathers.

When we come to consider libraries of
printed books in place of manuscripts, we
naturally find a greater variety of subjects
collected by the famous men who have
formed collections.   Montaigne, the friend
of all literary men, could not have been
the man we know him to have been if he
had not lived among his books.   Like many
a later book-lover, he decorated his library
with mottoes, and burnt-in his inscriptions

letter by letter with his own hands. Grotius made his love of books do him a special service, for he escaped from prison in a box which went backwards and forwards with an exchange of books for his entertainment and instruction.

Grolier and De Thou stand so pre-eminent among book collectors, and from the beauty of the copies they possessed the relics of their libraries are so frequently seen, that it seems merely necessary here to mention their names. But as Frenchmen may well boast of these men, so Englishmen can take pride in the possession of the living memory of Archbishop Parker, who enriched Cambridge, and of Sir Thomas Bodley, who made the Library at Oxford one of the chief glories of our land.

Old Lists of Books are always of interest to us as telling what our forefathers cared to have about them, but it is seldom that a list is so tantalising as one described by Mr. Edward Edwards in his *Libraries and Founders of Libraries*. Anne of Denmark presented her son Charles with a splendid series of volumes, bound in crimson and purple velvet. Abraham van der Dort, who was keeper of Charles's cabinet, made an inventory of this cabinet; and having no notion of how to make a catalogue of books, he has managed to leave out all the information we wish for. The inventory is among the Harleian MSS. (4718), and the following are specimens of the entries:—

> " Im'pris 19 books in Crimson velvet, whereof 18 are bound 4to. and ye 19th in folio, adorn'd with some silver guilt plate, and ye 2 claspes wanting. Given to ye King by Queen Ann of famous memory.
>
> Item, more 15 books, 13 thereof being in long 4to. and ye 2 lesser cover'd over also with purple velvet. Given also to ye King by ye said Queen Ann."

Most of the famous private libraries of days gone by have left little record of their existence, but Evelyn's collection is still carefully preserved at Wotton, the house of the Diarist's later years, and Pepys's books

continue at Cambridge in the cases he had
made for them, and in the order he fixed
for them. In a long letter to Pepys, dated
from Sayes Court, 12th August, 1689, Evelyn
gives an account of such private libraries
as he knew of in England, and in London
more particularly. He first mentions Lord
Chancellor Clarendon, to whom he dedicated his translation of Naudé's Advice,
and who "furnished a very ample library."
Evelyn observes that England was peculiarly defective in good libraries: "Paris
alone, I am persuaded, being able to show
more than all the three nations of Great
Britain." He describes Dr. Stillingfleet's,
at Twickenham, as the very best library.[1]
He did not think much either of the Earl
of Bristol's or of Sir Kenelm Digby's books,
but he says Lord Maitland's "was certainly
the noblest, most substantial and accomplished library that ever passed under the
spear."

[1] Narcissus Marsh, Archbishop of Armagh, is
said to have given £2500 for Bishop Stillingfleet's
Library.

In a useful little volume published at London in 1739, and entitled, *A Critical and Historical Account of all the Celebrated Libraries in Foreign Countries, as well ancient as modern*, which is stated to be written by "a Gentleman of the Temple," are some " General Reflections upon the Choice of Books and the Method of furnishing Libraries and Cabinets." As these reflections are interesting in themselves, and curious as the views of a writer of the middle of the eighteenth century on this important subject, I will transfer them bodily to these pages.

" Nothing can be more laudable than forming Libraries, when the founders have no other view than to improve themselves and men of letters : but it will be necessary, in the first place, to give some directions, which will be of great importance towards effecting the design, as well with regard to the choice of books as the manner of placing to advantage : nor is it sufficient in this case, to be learned, since he who would have a collection worthy of the name of a library must of all things have a thorough knowledge of books, that he may distinguish such as are valuable from the trifling. He must likewise understand the price of Books, otherwise he may purchase some at too high a rate, and undervalue others: all which requires no small judgment and experience.

"Let us suppose, then, the founder possessed of all those qualifications, three things fall next under consideration.

"First, the number of books; secondly, their quality; and, lastly, the order in which they ought to be ranged.

"As to the quantity, regard must be had, as well to places as to persons; for should a man of moderate fortune propose to have a Library for his own use only, it would be imprudent in him to embarrass his affairs in order to effect it. Under such circumstances he must rather consider the usefulness than the number of books, for which we have the authority of Seneca, who tells us that a multitude of books is more

burthensome than instructive to the understanding.

"But if a private person has riches enough
for founding a Library, as well for his own
use as for the public, he ought to furnish
it with the most useful volumes in all arts
and sciences, and procure such as are
scarcest and most valuable, from all parts,
that the learned, of whom there are many
classes, may instruct themselves in what
may be useful to them, and may gratify
their enquiries. But as the condition and
abilities of such as would form Libraries
are to be distinguished, so regard must
likewise be had to places, for it is very
difficult to procure, or collect books in
some countries, without incredible expense;
a design of that kind would be impractic-
able in America, Africa, and some parts of
Asia; so that nothing can be determined
as to the number of books, that depending
entirely upon a variety of circumstances,
and the means of procuring them, as has
been observ'd before.

"As to the second topic, special care must

be taken in the choice of books, for upon
that alone depends the value of a Library.
We must not form a judgment of books
either by their bulk or numbers, but by their
intrinsic merit and usefulness. Alexander
Severus's Library consisted of no more than
four volumes, that is the works of Plato,
Cicero, Virgil, and Horace. Melanchthon
seems to have imitated that Prince, for his
collection amounted to four books only,
Plato, Pliny, Plutarch, and Ptolemy.

"There is another necessary lesson for
those who form designs of making libraries,
that is, that they must disengage themselves
from all prejudices with regard either to
ancient or modern books, for such a wrong
step often precipitates the judgment, without scrutiny or examination, as if truth and
knowledge were confined to any particular
times or places. The ancients and moderns
should be placed in collections, indifferently,
provided they have those characters we
hinted before.

"Let us now proceed to the third head,
the manner of placing books in such order,

as that they may be resorted to upon any emergency, without difficulty, otherwise they can produce but little advantage either to the owners or others.

"The natural method of placing books and manuscripts is to range them in separate classes or apartments, according to the science, art, or subject, of which they treat.

"Here it will be necessary to observe, that as several authors have treated of various subjects, it may be difficult to place them under any particular class; Plutarch, for instance, who was an historian, a political writer, and a philosopher. The most advisable method then is to range them under the head of Miscellaneous Authors, with proper references to each subject, but this will be more intelligible by an example.

"Suppose, then, we would know the names of the celebrated Historians of the ancients; nothing more is necessary than to inspect the class under which the historians are placed, and so of other Faculties. By this management, one set of miscellaneous authors will be sufficient, and may be resorted to with as much ease and expedition as those who have confined themselves to one subject. In choice of books regard must be had to the edition, character, paper and binding. As to the price, it is difficult to give any positive directions ; that of ordinary works is easily known, but as to such as are very scarce and curious, we can only observe that their price is as uncertain as that of medals and other monuments of antiquity, and often depends more on the caprice of the buyer than the intrinsic merit of the work, some piquing themselves upon the possession of things from no other consideration than their exorbitant price."

Dr. Byrom's quaint library is still preserved at Manchester in its entirety. Bishop Moore's fine collection finds a resting place in the University Library at Cambridge, and the relics of the Library of Harley, Earl of Oxford, a mine of manuscript treasure, still remain one of the chief glories of the British Museum. How much cause for regret is there that the library itself, which Osborne bought and Johnson described, did not also find a settled home, instead of being dispersed over the land.

It is greatly to the credit of the rich and busy man to spend his time and riches in the collection of a fine library, but still greater honour is due to the poor man who does not allow himself to be pulled down by his sordid surroundings. The once-famous small-coalman, Thomas Britton, furnishes a most remarkable instance of true greatness in a humble station, and one, moreover, which was fully recognized in his own day. He lived next door to St. John's Gate, Clerkenwell, and although he gained his living by selling coals from door to door, many persons of the highest station were in the habit of attending the musical meetings held at his house. He was an excellent chemist as well as a good musician, and Thomas Hearne tells us that he left behind him "a valuable collection of musick mostly pricked by himself, which was sold upon his death for near an hundred pounds," "a considerable collection of musical instruments which was sold for fourscore pounds,"

"not to mention the excellent collection of
printed books that he also left behind him,
both of chemistry and musick. Besides
these books that he left, he had some years
before his death (1714) sold by auction a
noble collection of books, most of them
in the Rosicrucian faculty (of which he
was a great admirer), whereof there is a
printed catalogue extant, as there is of
those that were sold after his death, which
catalogue I have by me (by the gift of my
very good friend Mr. Bagford), and have
often looked over with no small surprize
and wonder, and particularly for the great
number of MSS. in the before-mentioned
faculties that are specified in it."[1]

Dr. Johnson, although a great reader, was
not a collector of books. He was forced
to possess many volumes while he was
compiling his Dictionary, but when that
great labour was completed, he no longer
felt the want of them. Goldsmith, on the
other hand, died possessed of a considerable

[1] *Reliquiæ Hearnianæ*, by Bliss, 2nd edition, 1869,
vol. ii. p. 14.

number of books which he required, or had at some time required, for his studies. "The Select Collection of Scarce, Curious, and Valuable Books, in English, Latin, Greek, French, Italian, and other Languages, late the Library of Dr. Goldsmith, deceased," was sold on Tuesday, the 12th of July, 1774, and the Catalogue will be found in the Appendix to Forster's Life. There were 30 lots in folio, 26 in quarto, and 106 in octavo and smaller sizes. Among the books of interest in this list are Chaucer's Works, 1602; Davenant's Works, 1673; Camoens, by Fanshawe, 1655; Cowley's Works, 1674; Shelton's Don Quixote; Raleigh's History of the World, 1614; Bulwer's Artificial Changeling, 1653; Verstegan's Antiquities, 1634; Hartlib's Legacie, 1651; Sir K. Digby on the Nature of Bodies, 1645; Warton's History of English Poetry, 1774; Encyclopédie, 25 vols., 1770; Fielding's Works, 12 vols., 1766; Bysshe's Art of Poetry; Hawkins's Origin of the English Drama, 3 vols., 1773; Percy's Reliques, 3 vols., Dublin, 1766;

Sir William Temple's Works; and De Bure,
Bibliographie Instructive.

A catalogue such as this, made within
a few weeks of the death of the owner, cannot but have great interest for us. The
library could not have been a very choice
one, for there is little notice of bindings
and much mention of odd volumes. It was
evidently a working collection, containing
the works of the poets Goldsmith loved, and
of the naturalists from whom he stole his
knowledge.

Gibbon was a true collector, who loved
his books, and he must have needed them
greatly, working as he did at Lausanne
away from public libraries. After his death
the library was purchased by 'Vathek' Beck-
ford, but he kept it buried, and it was of
no use to any one. Eventually it was sold
by auction, a portion being bought for the
Canton, and another portion going to
America. There was little in the man
Gibbon to be enthusiastic about, but it is
impossible for any true book lover not to
delight in the thoroughness of the author

of one of the noblest books ever written. The fine old house where the *Decline and Fall* was written and the noble library was stored still stands, and the traveller may stroll in the garden so beautifully described by Gibbon when he walked to the historical *berceau* and felt that his herculean labour was completed. His heart must be preternaturally dull which does not beat quicker as he walks on that ground. The thought of a visit some years ago forms one of the most vivid of the author's pleasures of memory.

Charles Burney, the Greek scholar, is said to have expended nearly £25,000 on his library, which consisted of more than 13,000 printed volumes and a fine collection of MSS. The library was purchased for the British Museum for the sum of £13,500.

Charles Burney probably inherited his love of collecting from his father, for Dr. Burney possessed some twenty thousand volumes. These were rather an incumbrance to the Doctor, and when he moved to Chelsea Hospital, he was in

some difficulty respecting them. Mrs.
Chapone, when she heard of these troubles,
proved herself no bibliophile, for she ex-
claimed, "Twenty thousand volumes! bless
me! why, how can he so encumber himself? Why does he not burn half? for
how much must be to spare that never can
be worth his looking at from such a store!
and can he want to keep them all?"

The love of books will often form a tie
of connection between very divergent characters, and in dealing with men who have
formed libraries we can bring together the
names of those who had but little sympathy
with each other during life.

George III. was a true book collector,
and the magnificent library now preserved
in the British Museum owes its origin to
his own judgment and enthusiastic love for
the pursuit. Louis XVI. cared but little
for books until his troubles came thick
upon him, and then he sought solace from
their pages. During that life in the Temple
we all know so well from the sad reading
of its incidents, books were not denied to

the persecuted royal family. There was
a small library in the " little tower," and
the king drew up a list of books to be
supplied to him from the library at the
Tuileries. The list included the works of
Virgil, Horace, Ovid, and Terence; of
Tacitus, Livy, Cæsar, Marcus Aurelius,
Eutropius, Cornelius Nepos, Florus, Justin,
Quintus Curtius, Sallust, Suetonius and
Velleius Paterculus ; the *Vies des Saints,*
the *Fables de la Fontaine, Télèmaque,* and
Rollin's *Traité des Etudes.*[1]

The more we know of Napoleon, and
anecdotes of him are continually being
published in the ever-lengthening series
of French memoirs, the less heroic appears
his figure, but he could not have been
entirely bad, for he truly loved books. He
began life as an author, and would always
have books about him. He complained
if the printing was bad or the binding poor,
and said, " I will have fine editions and
handsome binding. I am rich enough for

[1] Edwards, *Libraries and Founders of Libraries,*
p. 115.

that."[1] Thus spoke the true bibliophile.
Mr. Edwards has collected much interesting information respecting Napoleon and
his libraries, and of his labours I here
freely avail myself. Bourrienne affirms that
the authors who chiefly attracted Napoleon
in his school days were Polybius, Plutarch,
and Arrian. "Shortly before he left France
for Egypt, Napoleon drew up, with his own
hand, the scheme of a travelling library,
the charge of collecting which was given
to John Baptist Say, the Economist. It
comprised about three hundred and twenty
volumes, more than half of which are
historical, and nearly all, as it seems, in
French. The ancient historians comprised
in the list are Thucydides, Plutarch, Polybius, Arrian, Tacitus, Livy, and Justin.
The poets are Homer, Virgil, Tasso, Ariosto,
the *Télèmaque* of Fénélon, the *Henriade* of
Voltaire, with Ossian and La Fontaine.
Among the works of prose fiction are the
English novelists in forty volumes, of course

[1] Edwards, *Libraries and Founders*, p. 136.

in translations, and the indispensable *Sorrows of Werter*, which, as he himself told Goethe, Napoleon had read through seven times prior to October, 1808. In this list the Bible, together with the *Koran* and the *Vedas*, are whimsically, but significantly, entered under the heading Politics and Ethics (Politique et Morale).[1]

Napoleon was not, however, satisfied with the camp libraries which were provided for him; the good editions were too bulky and the small editions too mean: so he arranged the plan of a library to be expressly printed for him in a thousand duodecimo volumes without margins, bound in thin covers and with loose backs. "In this new plan 'Religion' took its place as the first class. The Bible was to be there in its best translation, with a selection of the most important works of the Fathers of the Church, and a series of the best dissertations on those leading religious sects—their doctrines and their history—which have powerfully

[1] *Correspondance de Napoleon Ier*, IV. pp. 37, 38, quoted by Edwards, *Libraries and Founders*, p. 130.

influenced the world. This section was limited to forty volumes. The Koran was to be included, together with a good book or two on mythology. One hundred and forty volumes were allotted to poetry. The epics were to embrace Homer, Lucan, Tasso, *Telemachus*, and the *Henriade.* In the dramatic portion Corneille and Racine were of course to be included, but of Corneille, said Napoleon, you shall print for me ' only what is vital ' (ce qui est resté), and from Racine you shall omit ' *Les Frères ennemis,* the *Alexandre,* and *Les Plaideurs.* Of Crébillon, he would have only *Rhadamiste* and *Atrée et Thyeste.* Voltaire was to be subject to the same limitation as Corneille.'"[1] In prose fiction Napoleon specifies the *Nouvelle Héloïse* and Rousseau's *Confessions,* the masterpieces of Fielding, Richardson and Le Sage, and Voltaire's tales. Soon after this Napoleon proposed a much larger scheme for a camp library, in which history alone would occupy three thousand volumes.

[1] Edwards, *Libraries and Founders,* p. 133.

History was to be divided into these sections—I. Chronology and Universal History. II. Ancient History (*a.* by ancient writers, *b.* by modern writers). III. History of the Lower Empire (in like subdivisions). IV. History, both general and particular. V. The Modern History of the different States of Europe. The celebrated bibliographer Barbier drew up, according to the Emperor's orders, a detailed catalogue of the works which should form such a library. " He calculated that by employing a hundred and twenty compositors and twenty-five editors, the three thousand volumes could be produced, in satisfactory shape, and within six years, at a total cost of £163,200, supposing fifty copies of each book to be printed."[1] The printing was begun, but little was actually done, and in six years Napoleon was in St. Helena.

In his last island home Napoleon had a library, and he read largely, often aloud, with good effect. It is an interesting fact

---

[1] Edwards, *Libraries and Founders*, p. 135.

that among Napoleon's papers were found
some notes on Geography written when a
boy, and these close with the words—
"*Sainte-Hélène—petite ile.*"[1]

In recapitulating here the names of a
few of the famous men who have formed
libraries it will be necessary to divide them
into two classes, 1, those whose fame arises
from their habit of collecting, and 2, those
authors in whose lives we are so much
interested that the names of the books they
possessed are welcomed by us as indications
of their characters. What can be said of
the libraries of the Duke of Roxburghe, Earl
Spencer, Thomas Grenville, and Richard
Heber that has not been said often before?
Two of these have been dispersed over the
world, and two remain, one the glory of a
noble family, and the other of the nation,
or perhaps it would be more proper to say
both are the glory of the nation, for every
Englishman must be proud that the Spencer
Library still remains intact.

[1] Edwards, *Libraries and Founders*, p. 142.

4

Heber left behind him over 100,000 volumes, in eight houses, four in England and four on the Continent, and no record remains of this immense library but the volumes of the sale catalogues. Such whole-sale collection appears to be allied to madness, but Heber was no selfish collector, and his practice was as liberal as Grolier's motto. His name is enshrined in lasting verse by Scott :—

> " Thy volumes, open as thy heart,
>   Delight, amusement, science, art,
>   To every ear and eye impart ;
>   Yet who of all that thus employ them,
>   Can like the owner's self enjoy them ?—
>   But hark ! I hear the distant drum :
>   The day of Flodden Field is come—
>   Adieu, dear Heber ! life and health,
>   And store of literary wealth."
>   —MARMION, *Introduction to the Sixth Canto.*

The Duke of Sussex was a worthy successor of his father, George III., in the ranks of book-collectors, and his library is kept in memory by Pettigrew's fine catalogue.

Douce and Malone the critics, and Gough the antiquary, left their libraries to the Bodleian, and thus many valuable books are available to students in that much-loved resort of his at Oxford. Anthony Morris Storer, who is said to have excelled in everything he set his heart on and hand to, collected a beautiful library, which he bequeathed to Eton College, where it still remains, a joy to look at from the elegance of the bindings. His friend Lord Carlisle wrote of him—

> "Whether I Storer sing in hours of joy,
> When every look bespeaks the inward boy;
> Or when no more mirth wantons in his breast,
> And all the man in him appears confest;
> In mirth, in sadness, sing him how I will,
> Sense and good nature must attend him still."

Jacob Bryant the antiquary left his library to King's College, Cambridge. At one time he intended to have followed Storer's example, and have left it to Eton College, but the Provost offended him, and he changed the object of his bequest. It is said that when he was discussing the

matter, the Provost asked whether he would
not arrange for the payment of the carriage
of the books from his house to Eton.   He
thought this grasping, and King's gained
the benefit of his change of mind.

Among great authors two of the chief
collectors were Scott and Southey.   Scott's
library still remains at Abbotsford, and no
one who has ever entered that embodiment
of the great man's soul can ever forget it.
The library, with the entire contents of
the house, were restored to Scott in 1830
by his trustees and creditors, "As the best
means the creditors have of expressing
their very high sense of his most honour-
able conduct, and in grateful acknowledg-
ment of the unparalleled and most successful
exertions he has made, and continues to
make for them."   The library is rich in
the subjects which the great author loved,
such as Demonology and Witchcraft.   In
a volume of a collection of Ballads and
Chapbooks is this note written by Scott in
1810: "This little collection of stall tracts
and ballads was formed by me, when a boy,

from the baskets of the travelling pedlars.
Until put into its present decent binding,
it had such charms for the servants, that it
was repeatedly, and with difficulty, recovered
from their clutches. It contains most of
the pieces that were popular about thirty
years since, and I dare say many that could
not now be procured for any price."

It is odd to contrast the book-loving
tastes of celebrated authors. Southey cared
for his books, but Coleridge would cut the
leaves of a book with a butter knife, and
De Quincey's extraordinary treatment of
books is well described by Mr. Burton in
the *Book Hunter*. Charles Lamb's loving
appreciation of his books is known to all
readers of the delightful Elia.

Southey collected more than 14,000
volumes, which sold in 1844 for nearly
£3000. He began collecting as a boy,
for his father had but few books. Mr.
Edwards enumerates these as follows :
The *Spectator*, three or four volumes of
the *Oxford Magazine*, one volume of the
Freeholder's Magazine, and one of the *Town*

and Country Magazine, Pomfret's *Poems,* the *Death of Abel,* nine plays (including *Julius Cæsar, The Indian Queen,* and a translation of *Merope*), and a pamphlet.[1]

Southey was probably one of the most representative of literary men.   His feelings in his library are those of all book-lovers, although he could express these feelings in language which few of them have at command :—

> My days among the dead are passed ;
>   Around me I behold,
> Where'er these casual eyes are cast,
>   The mighty minds of old :
> My never-failing friends are they,
> With whom I converse day by day.
>
>
> With them I take delight in weal,
>   And seek relief in woe ;
> And while I understand and feel
>   How much to them I owe,
> My cheeks have often been bedewed
> With tears of thoughtful gratitude.

[1] *Libraries and Founders of Libraries,* p. 95.

My thoughts are with the dead ; with them
    I live in long-past years ;
Their virtues love, their faults condemn,
    Partake their hopes and fears,
And from their lessons seek and find
Instruction with a humble mind.

My hopes are with the dead ; anon
    My place with them will be
And I with them shall travel on
    Through all futurity ;
Yet leaving here a name, I trust,
That will not perish in the dust.

Mr. Henry Stevens read a paper or rather delivered an address at the meeting of the Library Association held at Liverpool in 1883, containing his recollections of Mr. James Lenox, the great American book collector. I had the pleasure of listening to that address, but I have read it in its finished form with even greater delight. It is not often that he who pleases you as a speaker also pleases you as writer, but Mr. Stevens succeeds in both. If more bibliographers could write their reminiscences with the same spirit that he does, we

should hear less of the dullness of bibliography. I strongly recommend my readers
to take an early opportunity of perusing
this paper in the Liverpool volume of the
Transactions of the Library Association.

Mr. Stevens, among his anecdotes of Mr.
Lenox, records that he "often bought dupli-
cates for immediate use, or to lend, rather
than grope for the copies he knew to be
in the stocks in some of his store rooms
or chambers, notably Stirling's *Artists of
Spain*, a high-priced book."

This is a common trouble to large book
collectors, who cannot find the books they
know they possess. The late Mr. Crossley
had his books stacked away in heaps, and
he was often unable to lay his hands upon
books of which he had several copies.

CHAPTER II.

How to Buy.

 DISCUSSION has arisen lately in bibliographical journals as to how best to supply libraries with their books, the main principle agreed upon being that it is the duty of the librarian to buy his books as cheaply as possible. Some of these views are stated by Mr. H. R. Tedder in a letter printed in the *Library Chronicle* for July, 1884 (vol. i. p. 120). It appears that Professor Dziatzko contends that the books should always be bought as cheaply as possible, but that Dr. Julius Petzholdt holds the opinion that the chief object of the librarian should be to get his books as early as possible and not to wait until they can be had at second-hand. Mr. Tedder thinks that the two

plans of rapidity of supply and cheapness
of cost can in some respect be united.   Of
course there can be no difference of opinion
in respect to the duty of the librarian to
get as much for his money as he can, but
there are other points which require to be
considered besides those brought forward
before a satisfactory answer to the question
—How to Buy? can be obtained.   There
are three points which seem to have been
very much overlooked in the discussion,
which may be stated here.   1. Is the
librarian's valuable time well occupied by
looking after cheap copies of books?   2.
Will not the proposed action on the part
of librarians go far to abolish the intelligent
second-hand bookseller in the same way
as the new bookseller 'has been well-nigh
abolished in consequence of large dis-
counts?   3. Will not such action prevent
the publication of excellent books on
subjects little likely to be popular?

1. Most librarians find their time pretty
well occupied by the ordinary duties of buying, arranging, cataloguing, and finding the

books under their charge, and it will be
generally allowed that the librarian's first
duty is to be in his library, ready to attend to
those who wish to consult him. Now the
value of his time can be roughly estimated for
this purpose in money, and the value of the
time spent in doing work which could be
as well or better done by a bookseller
should fairly be added to the cost of the
books.

2. It has hitherto been thought advisable
to have one or more second-hand booksellers attached to an important library,
from whom the librarian may naturally
expect to obtain such books as he requires.
Of course a man of knowledge and experience must be paid for the exercise of
these qualities, but the price of books is
so variable that it is quite possible that the
bookseller, from his knowledge, may buy the
required books cheaper than the librarian
himself would pay for them. As far as it is
possible to judge from the information given
us respecting the collection of libraries,
bookbuyers have little to complain of as to

the price paid by them to such respectable
booksellers as have acted as their agents.
Perhaps too little stress has been laid upon
that characteristic which is happily so
common among honest men, viz. that the
agent is as pleased to get wares cheap for
a good customer as for himself. Mr. Tedder
says in his letter, " For rarer books I still
consider it safer and cheaper in the long
run to cultivate business relations with one
or more second-hand booksellers, and pay
them for their knowledge and experience."
But is this quite fair, and is it not likely
that the rarer books will be supplied cheaper
if the bookseller is allowed to pay himself
partly out of the sale of the commoner
books, which it is now proposed the librarian shall buy himself? My contention is
that it is for the advantage of libraries that
intelligent booksellers, ready to place their
knowledge at the service of the librarians,
should exist, and it is unwise and un-
economic to do that which may cause
this class to cease to exist. Sellers of
books must always exist, but it is possible

to drive out of the trade those who do
it the most honour. We see what has
occurred in the new book trade, and
there can be little doubt that the book-
buyer loses much more than he gains by
the present system of discount. When the
bookseller could obtain sufficient profit by
the sale of new books to keep his shop
open, it was worth his while to take some
trouble in finding the book required; but
now that the customer expects to buy a
book at trade price, he cannot be surprised
if he does not give full particulars as to
the publisher of the book he requires if it
is reported to him as "not known." Those
only who, by taking a large quantity of
copies, obtain an extra discount, can make
new bookselling pay.

3. There are a large number of books
which, although real additions to literature,
can only be expected to obtain a small
number of readers and buyers. Some of these
are not taken by the circulating libraries,
and publishers, in making their calculations,
naturally count upon supplying some of the

chief libraries of the country. If these libraries wait till the book is second-hand, the number of sales is likely to be so much reduced that it is not worth while to publish the book at all, to the evident damage of the cause of learning.

It has been often suggested that an arrangement should be made by libraries in close proximity, so that the same expensive book should not be bought by more than one of the libraries. No doubt this is advantageous in certain circumstances, but in the case of books with a limited sale it would have the same consequence as stated above, and the book would not be published at all, or be published at a loss.

Selden wrote in his *Table Talk*: "The giving a bookseller his price for his books has this advantage; he that will do so, shall have the refusal of whatsoever comes to his hand, and so by that means get many things which otherwise he never should have seen." And the dictum is as true now as it was in his time.

Many special points arise for consideration

when we deal with the question—How
to buy at sales? and Mr. Edward Edwards
gives the following four rules for the guidance of the young book-buyer (*Memoirs of
Libraries*, vol. ii. p. 645):

1. The examination of books before the
sale, not during it. 2. A steady unin-
termittent bidding up to his predetermined
limit, for all the books which he wants,
from the first lot to the last; and—if there
be any signs of a "combination"—for a
few others which he may *not* want. 3. Careful avoidance of all interruptions and con-
versation; with especial watchfulness of
the hammer immediately after the disposal
of those especially seductive lots, which
may have excited a keen and spirited
competition. (There is usually on such
occasions a sort of "lull," very favourable
to the acquisition of good bargains.) 4.
The uniform preservation and storing up
of priced catalogues of all important sales
for future reference.

A case of conscience arises as to whether
it is fit and proper for two buyers to agree

not to oppose each other at a public sale.
Mr. Edwards says, "At the sales Lord
Spencer was a liberal opponent as well as
a liberal bidder.   When Mason's books
were sold, for example, in 1798, Lord
Spencer agreed with the Duke of Roxburghe
that they would not oppose each other, in
bidding for some books of excessive rarity,
but when both were very earnest in their
longings, "toss up, after the book was
bought, to see who should win it."   Thus
it was that the Duke obtained his unique,
but imperfect, copy of Caxton's *Historye
of Kynge Blanchardyn and Prince Eglantyne*,
which, however, came safely to Althorp
fourteen years later, at a cost of two
hundred and fifteen pounds; the Duke
having given but twenty guineas."[1]

It is easy to understand the inducement
which made these two giants agree not to
oppose each other, but the agreement was
dangerously like a "knock-out." Mr. Henry
Stevens (in his *Recollections of Mr. James*

[1] *Libraries and Founders of Libraries*, 1864, p. 404.

Lenox) boldly deals with this question, and condemns any such agreement. He writes, "Shortly after, in 1850, there occurred for sale at the same auction rooms a copy of '*Aratus, Phaenomena*,' Paris, 1559, in 4°, with a few manuscript notes, and this autograph signature on the title, 'Jo. Milton, Pre. 2*s.* 6*d.* 1631.'" This I thought would be a desirable acquisition for Mr. Lenox, and accordingly I ventured to bid for it as far as £40, against my late opponent for the Drake Map, but he secured it at £40 10*s.*, remarking that "Mr. Panizzi will not thank you for thus running the British Museum." "That remark," I replied, "is apparently one of your gratuities. Mr. Panizzi is, I think, too much a man of the world to grumble at a fair fight. He has won this time, though at considerable cost, and I am sure Mr. Lenox will be the first to congratulate him on securing such a prize for the British Museum." "I did not know you were bidding for Mr. Lenox." "It was not necessary that you should." "Perhaps at another time," said he, "we

may arrange the matter beforehand, so
as not to oppose each other." "Very
well," I replied, "if you will bring me a
note from Mr. Panizzi something to this
effect : 'Mr. Stevens, please have a knock-
out with the bearer, the agent of the British
Museum, on lot * *, and greatly oblige Mr.
John Bull and your obdt. servant, A. P.,'
I will consider the proposition, and if Mr.
Lenox, or any other of my interested correspondents, is not unwilling to combine
or conspire to rob or cheat the proprietors,
the 'thing' may possibly be done. Mean-
while, until this arrangement is concluded,
let us hold our tongues and pursue an
honest course."   That man never again
suggested to me to join him in a "knock-
out."

In another place Mr. Stevens relates his
own experience as to holding two com-
missions, and the necessity of buying the
book above the amount of the lowest of the
two. The circumstance relates to a copy
of the small octavo Latin edition of the
Columbus Letter, in eight leaves, at the first

Libri sale, Feb. 19, 1849. Mr. Stevens
writes, " Mr. Brown ordered this lot with
a limit of 25 guineas, and Mr. Lenox of
£25. Now as my chief correspondents had
been indulged with a good deal of liberty,
scarcely ever considering their orders completely executed till they had received the
books and decided whether or not they
would keep them, I grew into the habit
of considering all purchases my own until
accepted and paid for. Consequently when
positive orders were given, which was very
seldom, I grew likewise into the habit of
buying the lot as cheaply as possible, and
then awarding it to the correspondent who
gave the highest limit. This is not always
quite fair to the owner; but in my case it
would have been unfair to myself to make
my clients compete, as not unfrequently the
awarded lot was declined and had to go to
another. Well, in the case of this Columbus
Letter, though I had five or six orders, I
purchased it for £16 10s., and, accordingly,
as had been done many times before within
the last five or six years without a grumble,

I awarded it to the highest limit, and sent
the little book to Mr. John Carter Brown.
Hitherto, in cases of importance, Mr. Lenox
had generally been successful, because he
usually gave the highest limit.   But in this
case he rebelled.   He wrote that the book
had gone under his commission of £25,
that he knew nobody else in the transaction,
and that he insisted on having it, or he
should at once transfer his orders to some
one else.   I endeavoured to vindicate my
conduct by stating our long-continued
practice, with which he was perfectly well
acquainted, but without success.   He grew
more and more peremptory, insisting on
having the book solely on the ground that
it went under his limit.   At length, after
some months of negotiation, Mr. Brown,
on being made acquainted with the whole
correspondence, very kindly, to relieve me
of the dilemma, sent the book to Mr. Lenox
without a word of comment or explanation,
except that, though it went also below his
higher limit, he yielded it to Mr. Lenox
for peace. . . . . From that time I

resorted, in cases of duplicate orders from them, to the expedient of always putting the lot in at one bid above the lower limit, which, after all, I believe is the fairer way in the case of positive orders. This sometimes cost one of them a good deal more money, but it abated the chafing and generally gave satisfaction. Both thought the old method the fairest when they got the prize. But I was obliged, on the new system of bidding, to insist on the purchaser keeping the book without the option of returning it." There can be no doubt that the latter plan was the most satisfactory.

Some persons appear to be under the impression that whatever a book fetches at a public sale must be its true value, and that, as the encounter is open and public, too much is not likely to be paid by the buyer; but this is a great mistake, and prices are often realized at a good sale which are greatly in advance of those at which the same books are standing unsold in second-hand booksellers' shops.

Much knowledge is required by those who

wish to buy with success at sales. Books
vary greatly in price at different periods,
and it is a mistake to suppose, from the
high prices realized at celebrated sales,
which are quoted in all the papers, that
books are constantly advancing in price.
Although many have gone up, many others
have gone down, and at no time probably
were good and useful books to be bought
so cheap as now. If we look at old sale
catalogues we shall find early printed books,
specimens of old English poetry and the
drama, fetching merely a fraction of what
would have to be given for them now; but,
on the other hand, we shall find pounds then
given for standard books which would not
now realize the same number of shillings;
this is specially the case with classics.

The following passage from Hearne's
Diaries on the fluctuations in prices is of
interest in this connection :—"The editions
of Classicks of the first print (commonly
called *editones principes*) that used to go
at prodigious prices are now strangely
lowered; occasioned in good measure by

Mr. Thomas Rawlinson, my friend, being forced to sell many of his books, in whose auction these books went cheap, tho' English history and antiquities went dear: and yet this gentleman was the chief man that raised many curious and classical books so high, by his generous and courageous way of bidding."[1]

These first editions, however, realize large prices at the present time, as has been seen at the sale of the Sunderland Library. It is experience only that will give the necessary knowledge to the book buyer, and no rules laid down in books can be of any real practical value in this case. Persons who know nothing of books are too apt to suppose that what they are inclined to consider exorbitant prices are matters of caprice, but this is not so. There is generally a very good reason for the high price.

We must remember that year by year old and curious books become scarcer, and the

---

[1] *Reliquiæ Hearnianæ*, 1869, vol. ii. p. 158.

number of libraries where they are locked up increase; thus while the demand is greater, the supply diminishes, and the price naturally becomes higher. A unique first edition of a great author is surely a possession to be proud of, and it is no ignoble ambition to wish to obtain it.

CHAPTER III.

PUBLIC LIBRARIES.

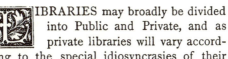IBRARIES may broadly be divided into Public and Private, and as private libraries will vary according to the special idiosyncrasies of their owners, so still more will public libraries vary in character according to the public they are intended for. The answer therefore to the question—How to form a Public Library?—must depend upon the character of the library which it is proposed to form. Up to the period when free town libraries were first formed, collections of books were usually intended for students; but when the Public Libraries' Acts were passed, a great change took place, and libraries being formed for general readers, and largely

with the object of fostering the habit of reading, an entirely new idea of libraries came into existence. The old idea of a library was that of a place where books that were wanted could be found, but the new idea is that of an educational establishment, where persons who know little or nothing of books can go to learn what to read. The new idea has naturally caused a number of points to be discussed which were never thought of before.

But even in Town Libraries there will be great differences. Thus in such places as Birmingham, Liverpool, and Manchester, the Free Libraries should be smaller British Museums, and in this spirit their founders have worked; but in smaller and less important towns a more modest object has to be kept in view, and the wants of readers, more than those of consulters of books, have to be considered.

Mr. Beriah Botfield has given a very full account of the contents of the libraries spread about the country and associated with the different Cathedrals in his *Notes on*

the Cathedral Libraries of England, 1849.
These libraries have mostly been formed
upon the same plan, and consist very largely
of the works of the Fathers, and of old
Divinity. Some contain also old editions
of the classics, and others fine early editions
of English authors. In former times these
libraries were much neglected, and many of
the books were lost; but the worst instance
of injury to a library occurred at Lincoln
at the beginning of the present century,
when a large number of Caxtons, Pynsons,
Wynkyn de Wordes, etc., were sold to Dr.
Dibdin, and modern books purchased for
the library with the proceeds. Dibdin
printed a list of his treasures under the title
of " The Lincolne Nosegay." Mr. Botfield
has reprinted this catalogue in his book.

The first chapter of the *United States
Report on Public Libraries* is devoted to
Public Libraries a hundred years ago.
Mr. H. E. Scudder there describes some
American libraries which were founded in
the last century. One of these was the
Loganian Library of Philadelphia. Here

is an extract from the will of James Logan,
the founder—

"In my library, which I have left to the
city of Philadelphia for the advancement
and facilitating of classical learning, are
above one hundred volumes of authors, in
folio, all in Greek, with mostly their versions.
All the Roman classics without exception.
All the Greek mathematicians, viz. Archi-
medes, Euclid, Ptolemy, both his Geography
and Almagest, which I had in Greek (with
Theon's Commentary, in folio, above 700
pages) from my learned friend Fabricius,
who published fourteen volumes of his
Bibliothèque Grecque, in quarto, in which,
after he had finished his account of Ptolemy,
on my inquiring of him at Hamburgh, how
I should find it, having long sought for it
in vain in England, he sent it to me out
of his own library, telling me it was so
scarce that neither prayers nor price could
purchase it; besides, there are many of the
most valuable Latin authors, and a great
number of modern mathematicians, with
all the three editions of Newton, Dr. Watts,

Halley, etc." The inscription on the house
of the Philadelphia Library is well worthy
of repetition here. It was prepared by
Franklin, with the exception of the reference to himself, which was inserted by the
Committee.

Be it remembered,
in honor of the Philadelphia youth
(then chiefly artificers),
that in MDCCXXXI
they cheerfully,
at the instance of BENJAMIN FRANKLIN,
one of their number,
instituted the Philadelphia Library,
which, though small at first,
is become highly valuable and extensively useful,
and which the walls of this edifice
are now destined to contain and preserve :
the first stone of whose foundation
was here placed
the thirty-first day of August, 1789.

Mr. F. B. Perkins, of the Boston Public
Library, contributed to the *Report on Public
Libraries in the United States* a useful chapter
on " How to make Town Libraries successful" (pp. 419-430). The two chief points

upon which he lays particular stress, and
which may be said to form the texts for
his practical remarks, are: (1) that a Public
Library for popular use must be managed
not only as a literary institution, but also
as a business concern; and (2) that it is a
mistake to choose books of too thoughtful
or solid a character. He says, "It is vain
to go on the principle of collecting books
that people ought to read, and afterwards
trying to coax them to read them. The
only practical method is to begin by supplying books that people already want to read,
and afterwards to do whatever shall be found
possible to elevate their reading tastes and
habits."

A series of articles on "How to Start
Libraries in Small Towns" was published
in the *Library Journal* (vol. i. pp. 161, 213,
249, 313, 355, 421), and Mr. Axon's *Hints
on the Formation of Small Libraries* has
already been mentioned. We must not be
too rigid in the use of the term Public
Libraries, and we should certainly include
under this description those institutional

Libraries which, although primarily intended for the use of the Members of the Societies to which they belong, can usually be consulted by students who are properly introduced.

Of Public Libraries first in order come the great libraries of a nation, such as the British Museum. These are supplied by means of the Copyright Law, but the librarians are not from this cause exonerated from the troubles attendant on the formation of a library. There are old books and privately printed and foreign books to be bought, and it is necessary that the most catholic spirit should be displayed by the librarians. The same may be said in a lesser degree of the great libraries of the more important towns.

In England the Universities have noble libraries, more especially those of Oxford and Cambridge, but although some colleges possess fine collections of books, college libraries are not as a rule kept up to a very high standard. The United States Report contains a full account of the college libraries in America (pp. 60–126).

The libraries of societies are to a large extent special ones, and my brother, the late Mr. B. R. Wheatley, in a paper read before the Conference of Librarians, 1877, entitled " Hints on Library Management, so far as relates to the Circulation of Books," particularly alluded to this fact. He wrote, " Our library is really a medical and surgical section of a great Public Library. Taking the five great classes of literature, I suppose medicine and its allied sciences may be considered as forming a thirtieth of the whole, and, as our books number 30,000, we are, as it were, a complete section of a Public Library of nearly a million volumes in extent."

The United States Report contains several chapters on special libraries, thus chapter 2 is devoted to those of Schools and Asylums; 4, to Theological Libraries; 5, to Law; 6, to Medical; and 7, to Scientific Libraries. For the formation of special libraries, special bibliographies will be required, and for information on this subject reference should be made to Chapter VI. of the present work.

When we come to deal with the Free
Public Libraries, several ethical questions
arise, which do not occur in respect to
other libraries. One of the most pressing
of these questions refers to the amount of
Fiction read by the ordinary frequenters
of these libraries.

This point is alluded to in the United
States Report on Public Libraries. Mr. J.
P. Quincy, in the chapter on Free Libraries
(p. 389), writes, " Surely a state which lays
heavy taxes upon the citizen in order that
children may be taught to read is bound to
take some interest in what they read; and
its representatives may well take cognizance
of the fact that an increased facility for
obtaining works of sensational fiction is not
the special need of our country at the close
of the first century of its independence."
He mentions a free library in Germanstown,
Pa., sustained by the liberality of a religious
body, and frequented by artisans and working people of both sexes. It had been
in existence six years in 1876, and then
contained 7000 volumes. No novels are

6

admitted into the library. The following is a passage from the librarian's report of 1874: "In watching the use of our library as it is more and more resorted to by the younger readers of our community, I have been much interested in its influence in weaning them from a desire for works of fiction. On first joining the library, the new comers often ask for such books, but failing to procure them, and having their attention turned to works of interest and instruction, in almost every instance they settle down to good reading and cease asking for novels. I am persuaded that much of this vitiated taste is cultivated by the purveyors to the reading classes, and that they are responsible for an appetite they often profess to deplore, but continue to cater to, under the plausible excuse that the public will have such works."

Mr. Justin Winsor in chapter 20 (Reading in Popular Libraries) expresses a somewhat different view. He writes, "Every year many young readers begin their experiences with the library. They find all the instructive reading they ought to have in their school books, and frequent the library for story books. These swell the issues of fiction, but they present the statistics of that better reading into which you have allured the older ones, from telling as they should in the average."

At the London Conference of Librarians (1877), Mr. P. Cowell, Librarian of the Liverpool Public Library, read a paper on the admission of Fiction in Free Public Libraries, where he discussed the subject in a very fair manner, and deplored the high percentage of novel reading in these libraries. At the Second Annual Meeting of the Library Association (1879) Mr. J. Taylor Kay, Librarian of Owens College, Manchester, in his paper on the Provision of Novels in Rate-supported Libraries, more completely condemned this provision. He concluded his paper with these words: " Clearly a hard and fast line must be drawn. A distinct refusal by the library committees to purchase a single novel or tale would be appreciated by the rate-payers. The suggestion of a sub-committee to read this literature would not be tolerated, and no man whose time is of value would undergo the infliction. The libraries would attain their true position, and the donations would certainly be of a higher class, if the aims of the committees were known to be higher. Manchester has already curtailed its issues of novels. It has been in the vanguard on the education question: and let us hope it will be true to its traditions, to its noble impulses, and lead the van in directing the educational influence of the free libraries, and striking out altogether any expenditure in the dissemination of this literature."

This question probably would not have come to the front if it were not that the educational value of Free Libraries, as the complement of Board Schools, has been very properly put forward by their promoters. With this aim in view, it does startle one somewhat to see the completely disproportionate supply of novels in the Free Libraries. This often rises to 75 per cent. of the total supply, and in some libraries

even a higher percentage has been reached.
There are, however, exceptions. At the
Baltimore Peabody Institute Fiction did
not rise to more than one-tenth of the total
reading. The following are some figures
of subjects circulated at that library above
1000 :—

Belles Lettres	4598
Fiction.	3999
Biography	2003
Greek and Latin Classics . . .	1265
History (American).	1137
Law.	1051
Natural History	1738
Theology	1168
Periodicals (Literary)	4728
Periodicals (Scientific). . . .	1466

Mr. Cowell says that during the year
ending 31st August, 1877, 453,585 volumes
were issued at the reference library alone
(Liverpool Free Public Library); of these
170,531 were strictly novels. The high-
percentage of novel reading is not confined
to Free Public Libraries, for we find that in
the Odd Fellows' Library of San Francisco,

in 1874, 64,509 volumes of Prose Fiction were lent out of a total of 78,219. The other high figures being Essays, 2280; History, 1823; Biography and Travels, 1664. In the College of the City of New York, of the books taken out by students between Nov. 1876, and Nov. 1877, 1043 volumes were Novels, the next highest numbers were Science, 153; Poetry, 133; History, 130.[1]

In considering this question one naturally asks if the masterpices of our great authors, which every one should read, are to be mixed up with the worthless novels constantly being published in the condemnation of Fiction; but, to some extent, both Mr. Cowell and Mr. Kay answer this. The first of these gentlemen writes: "As to the better class novels, which are so graphic in their description of places, costumes, pageantry, men, and events, I regret to say that they are not the most popular with those who stand in need of their instructive

---

[1] *Library Journal*, vol. ii. p. 70.

descriptions. I could generally find upon
the library shelves 'Harold,' 'The Last of
the Barons,' 'Westward Ho!' 'Hypatia,'
'Ivanhoe,' 'Waverley,' 'Lorna Doone,' etc.,
when not a copy of the least popular of
the works of Mrs. Henry Wood, 'Ouida,'
Miss Braddon, or Rhoda Broughton were
to be had." Mr. Kay corroborates this
opinion in his paper.

Most of us recognize the value of honest fiction for children and the overwrought brains
of busy men, but the reading of novels of
any kind can only be justified as a relaxation,
and it is a sad fact that there is a large class
of persons who will read nothing but novels
and who call all other books dry reading.
Upon the minds of this class fiction has a
most enervating effect, and it is not to be expected that ratepayers will desire to increase
this class by the indiscriminate supply of
novels to the Free Libraries. Some persons
are so sanguine as to believe that readers
will be gradually led from the lower species
of reading to the higher; but there is little
confirmation of this hope to be found in

the case of the confirmed novel readers we
see around us.

The librarian who, with ample funds for
the purpose, has the duty before him of
forming a Public Library, sets forward on
a pleasant task. He has the catalogues of
all kinds of libraries to guide him, and he
will be able to purchase the groundwork
of his library at a very cheap rate, for
probably at no time could sets of standard
books be bought at so low a price as now.
Many books that are not wanted by private
persons are indispensable for a Public
Library, and there being little demand for
them they can be obtained cheap. When
the groundwork has been carefully laid, then
come some of the difficulties of collecting.
Books specially required will not easily be
obtained, and when they are found, the
price will probably be a high one. Books
of reference will be expensive, and as these
soon get out of date, they will frequently
need renewal.

CHAPTER IV.

PRIVATE LIBRARIES.

REATING of private libraries, it will be necessary to consider their constitution under two heads, according as they are required in town or country. In London, for instance, where libraries of all kinds are easily accessible, a man need only possess books on his own particular hobby, and a good collection of books of reference; but in the country, away from public libraries, a well-selected collection of standard books will be necessary.

1. *Town.*

Every one who loves books will be sure to have some favourite authors on special subjects of study respecting which he needs

no instruction farther than that which is
ready to his hand. Books on these subjects
he will need, both in town and country, if
he possesses two houses. Some collectors
make their town house a sort of gathering-
place for the accessions to their country
libraries. Here a class is completed, bound,
and put in order, and then sent to the
country to find its proper place in the family
library.

This is an age of books of reference, and
as knowledge increases, and the books
which impart it to readers become un-
wieldy from their multitude, there are sure
to be forthcoming those who will reduce
the facts into a handy form. I have gathered
in the following pages the titles of some
of the best books of reference which are to
be obtained. Many, if not all of these, are
to be found in that magnificent library of
reference—the Reading Room of the British
Museum. In some cases where the books
are constantly being, reprinted, dates have
been omitted. There are, doubtless, many
valuable works which I have overlooked,

and some Text-books I have had to leave out owing to the exigencies of space, but I trust that the present list will be found useful.

Abbreviations. — Dictionnaire des Abréviations Latines et Françaises usitées dans les inscriptions lapidaires et métalliques, les manuscrits et les chartes du Moyen Age. Par L. Alph. Chassant. Quatrième édition. Paris, 1876. Sm. 8vo.

Anthropology.—Notes and Queries on Anthropology, for the use of Travellers and Residents in Uncivilized Lands. Drawn up by a Committee appointed by the British Association. London, 1874. Sm. 8vo.

Antiquities.—Dictionary of Greek and Roman Antiquities. Edited by Dr. William Smith. Roy. 8vo.

———— Dictionnaire des Antiquités Grecques et Romaines d'après les textes et les Monuments . . Ouvrage redigé . . sous la direction de Ch. Daremberg et Edm. Saglio. Paris, 1873. 4to.

———— The Life of the Greeks and Romans described from Antique Monuments, by E. Guhl and W. Koner, translated from the third German edition by F. Hueffer. London, 1875. 8vo.

———— Gallus or Roman Scenes of the Time of Augustus. By W. A. Becker, translated by F. Metcalfe. London.

———— Charicles : Illustrations of the Private Life of the Ancient Greeks. By W. A. Becker, translated by F. Metcalfe. London.

Antiquities.—Archæological Index to remains of antiquity of the Celtic, Romano-British and Anglo-Saxon Periods. By John Yonge Akerman. London, 1847. 8vo.

———— Introduction to English Antiquities. By James Eccleston. London, 1847. 8vo.

———— The English Archæologist's Handbook. By Henry Godwin. Oxford, 1867. 8vo.

Architecture.—A Dictionary of the Architecture and Archæology of the Middle Ages. . . . By John Britton. London, 1838.

———— History of Architecture in all countries, from the earliest times to the present day. By James Fergusson. London, 1865–76. 4 vols. 8vo.

———— Nicholson's Dictionary of the Science and Practice of Architecture, Building, Carpentry, etc. New edition, edited by Edward Lomax and Thomas Gunyon. London. 2 vols. 4to.

———— An Encyclopædia of Architecture, historical, theoretical, and practical. By Joseph Gwilt, revised by Wyatt Papworth. New edition. London, 1876. 8vo.

———— The Dictionary of Architecture, issued by the Architectural Publication Society. A to Oz. 4 vols. Roy. 4to. (In progress.)

———— A Glossary of Terms used in Grecian, Roman, Italian, and Gothic Architecture. Fifth edition, enlarged. Oxford, 1850. 3 vols. 8vo.

———— An Encyclopædia of Cottage, Farm, and Villa Architecture and Furniture. . . . By J. C. Loudon. London, 1833. 8vo.

Arts, Manufactures, etc.—Ure's Dictionary of Arts, Manufactures, and Mines, containing a clear exposition of their Principles and Practice. By Robert Hunt, assisted by F. W. Rudler. Seventh edition. London, 1875. 3 vols. 8vo.

——— Spons' Encyclopædia of the Industrial Arts, Manufactures, and Commercial Products. London, 1879. 8 vols. Roy. 8vo.

Astronomy.—History of Physical Astronomy. By Robert Grant. London [1852]. A most valuable book, but now out of print and scarce.

——— An Historical Survey of the Astronomy of the Ancients. By G. Cornewall Lewis. London, 1862. 8vo.

Bible.—Dictionary of the Bible, comprising its Antiquities, Biography, Mythology, and Geography. By Dr. William Smith. Roy. 8vo.

——— A Biblical Cyclopædia or Dictionary of Eastern Antiquities, Geography, Natural History, Sacred Annals and Biography, Theology and Biblical Literature, illustrative of the Old and New Testaments. Edited by John Eadie, D.D., LL.D. Twelfth edition. London, 1870. 8vo.

——— The Bible Atlas of Maps and Plans to illustrate the Geography and Topography of the Old and New Testaments and the Apocrypha, with Explanatory Notes by Samuel Clark, M.A. Also a complete Index of the Geographical Names . . by George Grove. London, 1868. 4to.

Bible. See *Concordances.*

Bibliography.—See Chapters V. and VI.

Biography.—Mr. Chancellor Christie contributed a very interesting article to the *Quarterly Review* (April, 1884) on Biographical Dictionaries, in which he details the history of the struggle between the publishers of the *Biographie Universelle* and Messrs. Didot, whose Dictionary was eventually entitled *Nouvelle Biographie Générale*. The new edition of the *Biographie Universelle* (45 vols. Imp. 8vo. Paris, 1854) is an invaluable work. Chalmers's Biographical Dictionary (32 vols. 8vo. 1812–17) is a mine of literary wealth, from which compilers have freely dug. Rose's (12 vols. 8vo. 1848) was commenced upon a very comprehensive plan, but the lives were considerably contracted before the work was completed. It is, however, a very useful work. L. B. Phillips's " Dictionary of Biographical Reference " contains 100,000 names, and gives the dates of birth and death, which in many instances is all the information the consulter requires, and should more be required, he is referred to the authority. This book is quite indispensable for every library. There are several national Biographical Dictionaries, and at last a thoroughly satisfactory Biographia Britannica is in course of publication by Messrs. Smith & Elder. The "Dictionary of National Biography, edited by Leslie Stephen," has reached the fifth volume, and extends to Bottisham.

—— Robert Chambers's Biographical Dictionary

of Eminent Scotsmen (Glasgow, 1835-56. 5 vols. 8vo.)
will be found useful.

Biography.—Dr. William Allen's "American Biographical Dictionary" was published at Boston in 1857.

—— Biographie Nouvelle des Contemporains
. . . Par A. V. Arnault [etc.]. Paris, 1820-25.
20 vols. 8vo. Mr. Edward Smith points this book
out to me as specially valuable for information respecting actors in the French Revolution.

—— Handbook of Contemporary Biography.
By Frederick Martin. London, 1870. Sm. 8vo.

—— Men of the Time : a Dictionary of Con-
temporaries. Eleventh edition. Revised by Thompson
Cooper. London, 1884. Sm. 8vo. A volume of
1168 pages should contain a fair representation of the
men of the day, and yet it is ludicrously incomplete.
The literary side is as much overdone as the scientific
side is neglected. This is not the place to make a list
of shortcomings, but it will probably astonish most
of our readers to learn that such eminent Men of the
Time as Sir Frederick Abel, Sir Frederick Bramwell,
and the late Dr. W. B. Carpenter are not mentioned.
As this book has as a high reputation, the editor
should thoroughly revise it for a new edition.

—— Men of the Reign. A Biographical Dictionary of Eminent Characters of both Sexes, who
have died during the reign of Queen Victoria. Edited
by T. Humphry Ward. (Uniform with "Men of the
Time.") London, 1885.

Biography.—Dictionnaire Universel des Contemporains. . . . Par G. Vapereau. Cinquième edition. Paris, 1880. 8vo.

——— Supplément. Oct. 1881.

——— Biographie Nationale des Contemporains, redigée par une Société de Gens de Lettres sous la direction de M. Ernest Glaeser. Paris, 1878. Royal 8vo.

——— Dictionnaire Général de Biographie Contemporaine Française et Etrangère. Par Ad. Bitard. Paris, 1878. 8vo.

——— To this list of Contemporary Biography may be added the Indexes of Obituary Notices published by the Index Society.

(*Bishops.*)—Fasti Ecclesiæ Anglicanæ, or a Calendar of the principal Ecclesiastical Dignitaries in England and Wales, and of the chief officers in the Universities of Oxford and Cambridge, from the earliest time to the year 1715. Compiled by John Le Neve. Corrected and continued from 1715 to the present time by T. Duffus Hardy. Oxford, 1854. 3 vols. 8vo.

——— Fasti Ecclesiæ Hibernicæ. The Succession of the Prelates and Members of Cathedral Bodies in Ireland. By Henry Cotton, D.C.L. Dublin, 1847-60. 5 vols. 8vo.

(*Lawyers.*)—Lives of the Chief Justices of England. By John Lord Campbell. Second edition. London, 1858. 3 vols. 8vo.

——— Lives of the Lord Chancellors and Keepers

of the Great Seal of England. By John Lord Campbell.
Fourth edition. London, 1856. 10 vols. Sm. 8vo.
(*Scientific Men.*)—Poggendorff (J. C.). Biogra-
phisch-Literarisches Handwörterbuch zur Geschichte
der exacten Wissenschaften, enthaltend Nachweis-
ungen über Lebensverhältnisse und Leistungen von
Mathematikern, Astronomen, Physikern, Chemikern,
Mineralogen, Geologen u. s. w. aller Völker und
Zeiten. Leipzig, 1863. Roy. 8vo.

(*Cambridge.*)—Athenæ Cantabrigienses. By Charles
Henry Cooper, F.S.A., and Thompson Cooper.
Cambridge, 1858-61. Vol. I. 1500-1585. Vol. II.
1586-1609. 8vo.
———— Graduati Cantabrigienses, 1760-1856. Cura
Josephi Romilly, A.M. Cantabrigiæ, 1856.
———— Graduati Cantabrigienses, 1800-1884. Cura
Henrici Richardo Luard, S.T.P. Cantabrigiæ, 1884.
(*Oxford.*)—Athenæ and Fasti Oxonienses. By Ant.
à Wood. New edition, with Notes, Additions, and
Continuation by the Rev. Dr. P. Bliss. 4 vols. 4to.
1813-20.
———— Catalogue of all Graduates in the University
of Oxford, 1659-1850. Oxford, 1851. 8vo.
(*Dublin.*)—A Catalogue of Graduates who have
proceeded to degrees in the University of Dublin from
the earliest recorded Commencements to July, 1866,
with Supplement to December 16, 1868. Dublin,
1869. 8vo. Vol. II. 1868-1883. Dublin, 1884. 8vo

7

(*Eton.*)—Alumni Etonenses, or a Catalogue of the
Provosts and Fellows of Eton College and King's
College, Cambridge, from the Foundation in 1443 to
the Year 1797. By Thomas Harwood. Birmingham,
1797. 4to.

(*Westminster.*)—The List of the Queen's Scholars
of St. Peter's College, Westminster, admitted on that
Foundation since 1663, and of such as have been
thence elected to Christ Church, Oxford, and Trinity
College, Cambridge, from the Foundation by Queen
Elizabeth, 1561, to the present time. Collected by
Joseph Welch. A new edition . . . by an old King's
Scholar. London, 1852. Roy. 8vo.

———

Botany.—An Encyclopædia of Trees and Shrubs;
being the Arboretum et Fruticetum Britannicum
abridged . . . By J. C. Loudon. London, 1842. 8vo.

——— Loudon's Encyclopædia of Plants . . . New
edition corrected to the present time. Edited by Mrs.
Loudon. London, 1855. 8vo.

——— The Vegetable Kingdom; or the structure,
classification and uses of plants, illustrated upon the
natural system. By John Lindley, Ph.D., F.R.S.
Third edition. London, 1853. 8vo.

——— International Dictionary of Plants in Latin,
German, English and French, for Botanists, and
especially Horticulturists, Agriculturists, Students of
Forestry and Pharmaceutists, by Dr. William Ulrich.
Leipzig, 1872. 8vo.

Botany.—Topographical Botany : being Local and Personal Records towards shewing the distribution of British Plants traced through 112 counties and vice-counties of England, Wales and Scotland. By Hewett Cottrell Watson. Second edition, corrected and enlarged. London, 1883. 8vo.

The need of an authoritative list of Botanical names must be frequently felt by a large number of writers, those who have but little knowledge of the science even more than Botanists themselves. The following work will be found useful for this purpose, but there is reason to hope that a much larger and more exhaustive list will shortly be published, as Mr. Daydon Jackson, Secretary of the Linnean Society, is, we believe, now engaged upon such a work. "Nomenclator Botanicus seu Synonymia Plantarum Universalis . . . . Autore Ernesto Theoph. Steudel ; editio secunda, Stuttgartiæ et Tubingæ, 1841." Royal 8vo.

Cards.—Facts and Speculations on the Origin and History of Playing Cards. By William Andrew Chatto. London, 1848. 8vo.

———— A Descriptive Catalogue of Playing and other Cards in the British Museum, accompanied by a Concise General History of the Subject, and Remarks on Cards of Divination and of a Politico-Historical Character. By William Hughes Willshire, M.D. Printed by order of the Trustees, 1876. Royal 8vo.

Chemistry.—A Dictionary of Chemistry and the allied Branches of other Sciences, founded on that of the late Dr. Ure. By Henry Watts. 1863-68. 5 vols. 8vo. Supplement, 1872. Second Supplement, 1879. Third Supplement, 1879-81. 2 vols.

────── Handbook of Modern Chemistry, Inorganic and Organic, for the use of Students. By Charles Meymott Tidy, M.B., F.C.S. London, 1878. 8vo.

────── Handbook of Chemistry. By L. Gmelin. Trans. by H. Watts. London, 1848-67. 17 vols. 8vo.

────── Industrial Chemistry, based upon the German edition of Payen's "Précis de Chimie Industrielle," edited by B. H. Paul. London, 1878.

────── A Treatise on Chemistry. By [Sir] H. E. Roscoe and C. Schorlemmer. London. 8vo.

Coins.—A Numismatic Manual. By John Yonge Akerman, F.S.A. London, 1840. 8vo.

────── The Silver Coins of England arranged and described by E. Hawkins. London, 1841. 8vo.

────── The Gold Coins of England arranged and described, being a sequel to Mr. Hawkins's Silver Coins of England, by his grandson, Robert Lloyd Kenyon. London, 1880. 8vo.

Commerce.—A Dictionary, Practical, Theoretical, and Historical, of Commerce and Commercial Navigation. By the late J. R. McCulloch. Latest edition by A. J. Wilson. London, 1882. 8vo.

────── History of British Commerce, 1763-1870. By Leone Levi. London, 1872. 8vo.

Concordances.

Aristophanes.—A Complete Concordance to the Comedies and Fragments of Aristophanes. By Henry Dunbar, M.D. Oxford, 1883. 4to.

Bible.—A complete Concordance to the Holy Scriptures of the Old and New Testaments. By Alexander Cruden, M.A. London, 1737. 4to. Second edition 1761, third edition 1769 ; this is the last corrected by the author. Most of the Concordances published since are founded upon Cruden.

——— An Analytical Concordance to the Holy Scriptures, or the Bible presented under distinct and classified heads of topics. Edited by John Eadie, D.D., LL.D. London and Glasgow, 1856. 8vo.

Homer.—A Complete Concordance to the Iliad of Homer. By Guy Lushington Prendergast. London, 1875. 4to.

——— A Complete Concordance to the Odyssey and Hymns of Homer, to which is added a Concordance to the parallel passages in the Iliad, Odyssey and Hymns. By Henry Dunbar, M.D. Oxford, 1880. 4to.

Milton.—A Complete Concordance to the Poetical Works of Milton. By Guy Lushington Prendergast, Madras Civil Service. Madras, 1857. 4to. Originally published in 12 parts.

——— A Complete Concordance to the Poetical Works of John Milton. By Charles Dexter Cleveland, LL.D. London, 1867. Sm. 8vo.

The Rev. H. J. Todd compiled a verbal Index to the whole of Milton's Poetry, which was appended to the second edition of his life of the Poet (1809).

Pope.—A Concordance to the Works of Alexander Pope. By Edwin Abbott, with an Introduction by Edwin A. Abbott, D.D. London, 1875. Royal 8vo.

Shakespeare. — The Complete Concordance to Shakspere : being a verbal Index to all the passages in the dramatic works of the Poet. By Mrs. Cowden Clarke. London, 1845. Royal 8vo.

—— Shakespeare-Lexicon : a Complete Dictionary of all the English words, phrases and constructions in the works of the poet. By Dr. Alexander Schmidt. (Berlin and London), 1874. 2 vols. royal 8vo.

—— A Concordance to Shakespeare's Poems : an Index to every word therein contained. By Mrs. Horace Howard Furness. Philadelphia, 1874.

—— A Handbook Index to the Works of Shakespeare, including references to the phrases, manners, customs, proverbs, songs, particles, etc., which are used or alluded to by the great Dramatist. By J. O. Halliwell, Esq., F.R.S. London, 1866. 8vo. Only fifty copies printed.

Tennyson.—A Concordance of the entire works of Alfred Tennyson, P.L., D.C.L., F.R.S. By D. Barron Brightwell. London, 1869. 8vo.

Tennyson.—Concordance to the works of Alfred Tennyson, Poet Laureate. London, 1870. "The Holy Grail," etc., is indexed separately.

—— An Index to "In Memoriam." London, 1862.

Costume.—A Cyclopædia of Costume or Dictionary of Dress, including Notices of Contemporaneous Fashions on the Continent. . . . By James Robinson Planché, Somerset Herald. London, 1876-79. 2 vols. 4to. Vol. I. Dictionary. Vol. II. General History of Costume in Europe.

Councils.—Councils and Ecclesiastical Documents relating to Great Britain and Ireland. Edited after Spelman and Wilkins, by Arthur West Haddan, B.D., and William Stubbs, M.A. Oxford, 1869. Vol. II. Part I. 1873. Vol. III. 1871. 8vo.

—— England's Sacred Synods. A Constitutional History of the Convocations of the Clergy from the earliest Records of Christianity in Britain to the date of the promulgation of the present Book of Common Prayer, including a List of all Councils, Ecclesiastical as well as Civil, held in England in which the Clergy have been concerned. By James Wayland Joyce, M.A. London, 1855. 8vo.

Dates.—See *History.*

Dictionaries.

(*English.*)—One of the most useful English Dictionaries is the "Imperial Dictionary" by Ogilvie, which has been edited with great care by Charles Annandale.[1] The vocabulary is very full, the etymology is trustworthy, and the definitions are clear and satisfactory. The engravings which are interspersed with the text are excellent, and greatly add to the utility of the Dictionary.

For years preparations have been made for a Standard English Dictionary, and at last the work has been commenced under the able editorship of Dr. James A. H. Murray. In 1857, on the suggestion of Archbishop Trench, the Philological Society undertook the preparation of a Dictionary, "which by the completeness of its vocabulary, and by the application of the historical method to the life and use of words, might be worthy of the English language and of English scholarship." The late Mr. Herbert Coleridge and Dr. Furnivall undertook the editorship, and a large number of volunteers came forward to read books and extract quotations. Mr. Coleridge died in the midst of his work, and upon Dr. Furnivall devolved the entire editorship in addition to his other onerous duties as Secretary of the Philological Society. He projected the admirable system of subediting, which proved so successful. As the work proceeded several of the most energetic and most

---

[1] The Imperial Dictionary of the English Language: a Complete Encyclopædic Lexicon, Literary, Scientific, and Technological. By John Ogilvie, LL.D. New edition. Carefully revised and greatly augmented, edited by Charles Annandale, M.A. London, 1882-83. 4 vols. Imp. 8vo.

competent workers undertook to sub-edit the materials
already collected, each one taking a separate letter of the
alphabet. Some two million quotations were amassed,
but still the man was wanting who would devote his
life to forming the Dictionary from these materials.
In course of time Dr. Murray came forward, and in
1878 he prepared some specimens for submission to
the Delegates of the Clarendon Press, who agreed to
publish the Dictionary. The first part was published
in 1884, and the second in 1885.[1] It is hoped that in
future it will be possible to issue a part every six
months. At present the alphabet is carried down to
Batten. This is one of the most magnificent pieces of
work that has ever been produced in any country, and
it is an honour to every one concerned. To the
Philological Society who conceived it, to Dr. Murray
and his staff who have devoted so much labour and
intellect to its production, and to the Clarendon
Press who have published it to the world. It is,
moreover, an honour to the country which now possesses a well-grounded hope of having, at no distant
day, the finest Historical Dictionary ever produced.

In this connection the *Encyclopædic Dictionary*,
now in course of publication by Messrs. Cassell,
should be mentioned as a valuable work.

[1] A New English Dictionary on Historical Principles,
founded mainly on the materials collected by the Philological
Society. Edited by James A. H. Murray, LL.D., with the
assistance of many Scholars and Men of Science. Oxford,
Clarendon Press. Royal 4to.

Up to a few years ago it was impossible to obtain any satisfactory etymological information on English words from our Dictionaries. Mr. Hensleigh Wedgwood partly removed this reproach by the publication of his very valuable " Dictionary of English Etymology " in 1859,[1] but in this work Mr. Wedgwood only dealt with a portion of the vocabulary.

Professor Skeat commenced the publication of his indispensable "Etymological Dictionary of the English Language " (Clarendon Press) in 1879, and in 1884 he produced a second edition. In 1882 Professor Skeat published "A Concise Etymological Dictionary," which is something more than an abridgment, and a book which should find a place in all libraries of reference.

A Glossarial Index to the Printed English Literature of the Thirteenth Century. By H. Coleridge. London, 1859. 8vo. This was one of the earliest publications which grew out of the preparations for the great Philological Society's Dictionary. A new edition, prepared by Mr. H. Bradley, is about to be issued by the Clarendon Press. Stratmann's Dictionary of the Old English Language (third edition, Krefeld, 1878) is an indispensable work.

Of single volume Dictionaries, Mr. Hyde Clarke's "New and Comprehensive Dictionary of the English Language as spoken and written " in Weale's Educational Series (price 3*s.* 6*d.*) is one of the most

[1] A second edition appeared in 1871-72.

valuable. I have time after time found words there
which I have searched for in vain in more important
looking Dictionaries. Mr. Clarke claims that he was
the first to raise the number of words registered in an
English Dictionary to 100,000.

The Rev. James Stormonth's "Dictionary of the
English Language, Pronouncing, Etymological, and
Explanatory," is a work of great value. It is so
well arranged and printed that it becomes a pleasure
to consult it.

Those who are interested in Dialects will require
all the special Dictionaries which have been published, and these may be found in the Bibliography
now being compiled by the English Dialect Society,
but those who do not make this a special study will
be contented with "A Dictionary of Archaic and
Provincial Words, Obsolete Phrases, Proverbs, and
Ancient Customs, from the Fourteenth Century, by
J. O. Halliwell" (fifth edition, London, 1865, 2 vols.
8vo.), which is well-nigh indispensable to all. Nares's
Glossary (1822-46, new edition, by J. O. Halliwell
and T. Wright, 2 vols. 8vo. 1859) is also required
by those who make a study of Old English Literature.

The following is a short indication of some
of the most useful working Dictionaries:

Arabic.—Lane.

Greek.—Liddell & Scott's Greek-English Lexicon,
both in 4to. and in abridged form in square 12mo.

Latin.—The Clarendon Press publish a Latin Dictionary founded on Andrews's edition of Freund, and edited by C. T. Lewis and C. Short, which is of great value. Smith's Dictionary, both the large edition and the smaller one, and that of Riddle are good.

French.—The Dictionaries of Fleming and Tibbins, and Spiers, keep up their character, but for idioms the International French and English Dictionary of Hamilton and Legros is the best. For smaller Dictionaries Cassell's is both cheap and good. Bellows's Pocket Dictionary has obtained considerable fame, but those who use it need a good eyesight on account of the smallness of the type. It is, however, beautifully printed. The Standard French Dictionaries of that language alone are the noble work of Littré and the excellent Dictionary of Poitevin (2 vols. 4to.). For early French Godefroy's elaborate work, which is now in progress, must be consulted.

German.—Fluegel's German and English Dictionary still holds its own, but Koehler's Dictionary is also excellent. Hilpert's and Lucas's Dictionaries, both good ones, are now out of print. Of Standard German Dictionaries Grimm's great work is still in progress. Sanders's Dictionary is also of great value.

Danish and Norwegian.—The Dictionary by Ferrall, Repp, Rosing and Larsen is good.

Dutch.—Calisch (2 vols. 8vo. 1875).

Hebrew.—Fuerst, Gesenius.

Icelandic.—Vigfusson.

Italian.—Baretti's Dictionary still keeps up its character, but Millhouse's work is also good.

Portuguese.—Vieyra.

Russian.—Alexandrow.

Sanscrit.—Monier Williams. Boehtlingk and Roth.

Pâli.—Childers.

Spanish. – Neumann and Baretti, and also Velasquez.

Swedish.—Oman.

———

Drama.—Biographia Dramatica ; or a Companion to the Playhouse . . . originally compiled in the year 1764 by David Erskine Baker, continued thence to 1782 by Isaac Reed, and brought down to the end of November, 1811 . . . by Stephen Jones. London, 1812. 3 vols. 8vo.

——— A Dictionary of Old English Plays existing either in print or in manuscript, from the earliest times to the close of the seventeenth century ; by James O. Halliwell, Esq., F.R.S. London, 1860. 8vo.

Drugs.—Pharmacographia : a History of the Principal Drugs of Vegetable Origin met with in Great Britain and British India. By Friedrich A. Flückiger, Ph.D., and Daniel Hanbury, F.R.S. Second edition. London, 1879. 8vo.

Ecclesiology.—Dictionary of Doctrinal and Historical Theology. Edited by the Rev. J. H. Blunt, M.A. Second edition. London, 1872. Imp. 8vo.

Ecclesiology.—Dictionary of Christian Antiquities. By William Smith, LL.D., and Professor S. Cheatham. London, 1876-80. 2 vols. royal 8vo.

—— Dictionary of Sects, Heresies, Ecclesiastical Parties, and Schools of Religious Thought. Edited by the Rev. John Henry Blunt, M.A. London, 1874. Imp. 8vo.

—— Glossary of Ecclesiastical Ornament and Costume, compiled from Ancient Authorities and Examples. By A. Welby Pugin, Architect. . . . Enlarged and revised by the Rev. Bernard Smith, M.A. Third edition. London, 1868. 4to.

—— A Glossary of Liturgical and Ecclesiastical Terms. Compiled and arranged by the Rev. Frederick George Lee, D.C.L. London, 1877. Sq. 8vo.

—— See *Ritual.*

Encyclopædias.—The Encyclopædia Britannica, or a Dictionary of Arts, Sciences and General Literature. Ninth edition. Edinburgh, 1875. 4to. Now in course of publication.

—— Encyclopædia Metropolitana, or Universal Dictionary of Knowledge. . . . London, 1815-41. 26 vols. 4to.

—— Chambers's Encyclopædia. 10 vols. royal 8vo.

—— Dictionary of Science, Literature, and Art. By W. T. Brande. 1842. New edition, edited by the Rev. J. W. Cox. London, 1866-67. 3 vols. 8vo.

Encyclopædias.—Rees's Cyclopædia (39 vols., plates 6 vols. 1820, 4to.) can be bought excessively cheap, and is well worth a place in a library where room can be found for it, as many of its articles have never been superseded.

———— Grand Dictionnaire Universel du XIXᵉ Siècle Français, Historique, Géographique, Mythologique, Bibliographique, Littéraire, Artistique, Scientifique, etc. . . . Par Pierre Larousse. Paris, 1866-76. 15 vols. 4to. Supplément, tome 16, 1878.

———— Dictionnaire Universel des Sciences, des Lettres et des Arts . . . redigé avec la collaboration d'Auteurs spéciaux par M. N. Bouillet . . . douzième édition. Paris, 1877. 8vo.

Geography.—A General Dictionary of Geography, descriptive, physical, statistical, historical, forming a complete Gazetteer of the World. By A. Keith Johnston. New edition. London, 1877. 8vo.

———— The Library Cyclopædia of Geography, descriptive, physical, political and historical, forming a New Gazetteer of the World. By James Bryce, M. A. and Keith Johnston. London, 1880. Royal 8vo.

———— Index Geographicus, being a List alphabetically arranged of the principal places on the Globe, with the countries and sub-divisions of the countries in which they are situated and their latitudes and longitudes. Compiled specially with reference to Keith Johnston's Royal Atlas, but applicable to all modern atlases and maps. Edinburgh, 1864. Roy. 8vo.

Geography.—Etymologisch-Geographisches Lexikon. Separat-Ausgabe des lexikalischen Theils der Nomina Geographica von Dr. J. J. Egli. Leipzig, 1880. Royal 8vo.

———— Dictionary of Greek and Roman Geography, by various writers, edited by Dr. W. Smith. London, 1852. 2 vols. 8vo.

(*Scotland.*)—Ordnance Gazetteer of Scotland. A Survey of Scottish Topography, statistical, biographical and historical. Edited by Francis H. Groome. Edinburgh, 1884. Vol. I, roy. 8vo.

(*France.*)—Santini. Dictionnaire Général . . . des Communes de France et des Colonies. Paris. 8vo.

———— Dictionnaire des Postes de la République Française. 6e edition. Rennes, 1881. Roy. 8vo.

(*Italy.*)—Il Libro dé Comuni del Regno d'Italia. Compilato sopra elementi officiali da Achille Moltedo. Napoli, 1873. Roy. 8vo.

(*United States.*)—The National Gazetteer, a Geographical Dictionary of the United States . . . By L. de Colange, LL.D. London, 1884. Roy. 8vo.

(*India.*)—Cyclopædia of India and of Eastern and Southern Asia, Commercial, Industrial, and Scientific. . . . Edited by Edward Balfour. . . . Second edition. Madras, 1871-73. 5 vols. Roy. 8vo. Third edition. London, 1885. 3 vols. The first edition was published in 1858, and two Supplements in 1862.

Geology.—A Catalogue of British Fossils : comprising the Genera and Species hitherto described,

with references to their geological distribution. . . .
By John Morris, F.G.S. Second edition. London,
1854. 8vo.

Geology.—Principles of Geology. By Sir Charles
Lyell. 10th edition. London, 1867-8. 2 vols. 8vo.
—————— Manual of Elementary Geology. By Sir
Charles Lyell. London, 1865. 8vo.

History.—Blair's Chronological and Historical
Tables from the Creation to the present times. . . .
[Edited by Sir Henry Ellis.] Imp. 8vo. London,
1844.
—————— Atlas Universel d'Histoire et de Géographie
contenant 1e la Chronologie. . . . 2e la Généologie
. . . 3e la Géographie. . . . Par M. N. Bouillet.
Deuxième édition. Paris, 1872. 8vo.
—————— Dictionnaire Universel d'Histoire et de
Géographie contenant 1e l'Histoire proprement dite.
. . . 2e la Biographie Universelle. . . . 3e la Mytho-
logie. . . . 4e la Géographie ancienne et moderne.
Par M. N. Bouillet . . . ouvrage revu et continué
par A Chassang. Nouvelle édition (vingt-cinquième),
avec un Supplement. Paris, 1876. 8vo.
—————— The Map of Europe by Treaty, showing
the various political and territorial changes which
have taken place since the General Peace of 1814,
with numerous maps and notes. By Edward Hertslet,
C.B. London, 1875. Vol. 1, 1814-1827; vol. 2,
1828-1863; vol. 3, 1864-1875.—This work shows
the changes which have taken place in the Map of

Europe by Treaty or other International arrangements.
It contains a List of Treaties, etc., between Great
Britain and Foreign Powers for the maintenance of
the Peace of Europe and for the Settlement of
European Questions, 1814-75.

History.—Moniteur des Dates, contenant un million
des renseignements biographiques, généalogiques et
historiques. Par Edouard Oettinger. Dresde, 1866-68.
6 thin vols.   4to.   Tomes 7, 8, 9, Supplément
commencé par E. M. Oettinger considérablement
augmenté . . . par Dr. Hugo Schramm.   Leipzig,
1873-1882.

—— Haydn's Dictionary of Dates and Universal
Information relating to all Ages. 16th edition, by
Benjamin Vincent. London.

—— The Manual of Dates.   A Dictionary of
Reference of the most important facts and events in
the History of the World.   By George H. Townsend.
Fifth edition entirely remodelled and edited by
Frederick Martin.   London, 1877.   8vo.

—— Encyclopædia of Chronology, Historical
and Biographical.   By B. B. Woodward, B.A , and
William L. R. Cates.   London, 1872.   8vo.

—— The Dictionary of Chronology, or Historical
and Statistical Register.   Compiled and edited by
William Henry Overall, F.S.A.   London, 1870. 8vo.

—— The Anniversary Calendar, Natal Book,
and Universal Mirror ; embracing anniversaries of
persons, events, institutions, and festivals, of all

denominations, historical, sacred and domestic, in every period and state of the world. London, 1832. 2 vols. 8vo.

History.—An Epitome of the Civil and Literary Chronology of Rome and Constantinople, from the death of Augustus to the death of Heraclius. By Henry Fynes Clinton, M.A. Edited by the Rev. C. J. Fynes Clinton, M.A. Oxford, 1853. 8vo.

———— Fasti Romani : the Civil and Literary Chronology of Rome and Constantinople, from the death of Augustus to the death of Justin II. [to the death of Heraclius]. By Henry Fynes Clinton, M.A. Oxford, 1845-50. 2 vols. 4to.

———— Fasti Hellenici : the Civil and Literary Chronology of Greece, from the earliest accounts to the death of Augustus. By Henry Fynes Clinton, M.A. Oxford, 1834-51. 3 vols. 4to.

———— Descriptive Catalogue of Materials relating to the History of Great Britain and Ireland to the end of the reign of Henry VII. By Thomas Duffus Hardy. London, 1862–71. Vol. I. From the Roman Period to the Norman Invasion. Vol. II. A.D. 1066 to A.D. 1200. Vol. III. A.D. 1200 to A.D. 1327.

———— The Dictionary of English History. Edited by Sidney J. Low, B.A., and F. S. Pulling, M.A. London, 1884. 8vo.

———— Introduction to the Study of English History. By Samuel R. Gardiner, Hon. LL.D., and

J. Bass Mullinger, M.A. London, 1881. 8vo. The Second part by Mr. Mullinger is devoted to Authorities, and is a model of what such a work should be.

History.—Handy-Book of Rules and Tables for Verifying Dates with the Christian Era . . . with Regnal years of English Sovereigns from the Norman Conquest to the present time, A.D. 1066 to 1874. By John J. Bond. London, 1875. Sm. 8vo.

———— The Annals of England : an Epitome of English History, from contemporary writers, the Rolls of Parliament and other Public Records. Library Edition. Oxford and London, 1876. 8vo. Contains some valuable information as to the sources of history in the Appendix.

———— The Representative History of Great Britain and Ireland, being a History of the House of Commons and of the Counties, Cities, and Boroughs of the United Kingdom from the earliest period. By T. H. B. Oldfield. London, 1816. 6 vols. 8vo.

———— An Index to "The Times," and to the topics and events of the year 1862. [By J. Giddings.] London, 1863. 8vo.

———— An Index to "The Times," and to the topics and events of the year 1863. By J. Giddings. London, 1864. 8vo.

———— Index to "The Times" Newspaper, 1864, to September, 1885. London. 4to.

———— Annals of our Time, from the accession of Queen Victoria, 1837, to the Peace of Versailles, 1871.

By J. Irving. London, 1871. 8vo. Supplement
(Feb. 1871—July, 1878). London, 1879. 8vo.
(*France.*)—Dictionnaire Historique de la France
. . . Par Ludovic Lalanne. Paris, 1872. 8vo.

———

Insurance.—The Insurance Cyclopædia, being a
Dictionary of the definition of terms used in connexion
with the theory and practice of Insurance in all its
branches ; a Biographical Summary . . . a Bibliographical Reportery . . . By Cornelius Walford.
London, vol. 1, 1871, to vol. 6. Royal 8vo.

Language.—See *Dictionaries*, *Philology*.

Law.—The Law-Dictionary, explaining the rise,
progress, and present state of the British Law . . .
By Sir Thomas Edlyne Tomlins ; fourth edition by
Thomas Colpitts Granger. London, 1835. 2 vols. 4to.

——— Wharton's Law-Lexicon, forming an Epitome
of the Law of England . . . seventh edition by J. M.
Lely, M.A. London, 1863. Royal 8vo.

——— A Law Dictionary, adapted to the Constitution and Laws of the United States of America and
of the several States of the American Union . . . By
John Bouvier. Fourteenth edition. Philadelphia, 1870.

——— The Lawyer's Reference Manual of Law
Books and Citations. By Charles C. Soule. Boston,
1883. 8vo.

——— Ancient Law ; its connection with the early
history of Society, and its relation to modern ideas.
By H. S. Maine. London, 1861. 8vo.

Law.—Lectures in Jurisprudence. By John Austin. Third edition, revised and edited by R. Campbell. London, 1869. 3 vols. 8vo.

—————— Justice of the Peace and Parish Officer. By R. Burn. The 30th edition was published in 1869. The 13th edition of Archbold's Justice of the Peace appeared in 1878.

—————— Blackstone's Commentaries on the Laws of England. Student's edition.

Literature.

(*English.*) — Cyclopædia of English Literature. Edited by Robert Chambers. Edinburgh, 1843. New edition by Robert Carruthers. Edinburgh. 2 vols. Royal 8vo.

—————— Dictionary of English Literature, being a Comprehensive Guide to English Authors and their Works. By Davenport Adams. London, n.d. Sq. 8vo.

—————— Professor Henry Morley's *English Writers,* his *Fables of English Literature,* and his volumes of Selections, entitled *Library of English Literature,* will be found of great value.

(*American.*)—Cyclopædia of American Literature : embracing personal and critical Notices of Authors, and selections from their writings . . . By Evert A. Duyckinck and George L. Duyckinck. Edited to date by M. Laird Simons. Philadelphia, 1877. 2 vols. Imp. 8vo.

—————— The Poets and Poetry of Europe, with

Introductions and Biographical Notices, by Henry
Wadsworth Longfellow. London, 1855. Roy. 8vo.

(*Polish.*)—Bentkowskiego (F.). Historya Literatury
Polskiey. Warszawie, 1814. 2 vols. 8vo.

(*Russian.*)—Otto (Friedrich). History of Russian
Literature, with a Lexicon of Russian Authors.
Translated from the German by George Cox. Oxford,
1839. 8vo.

(*Spanish.*)—Ticknor (George). History of Spanish
Literature. New York, 1849. 3 vols. 8vo.

(*Classical.*)—A History of Latin Literature from
Ennius to Boethius. By George Augustus Simcox,
M.A. London, 1883. 2 vols. 8vo.

———— A History of Roman Classical Literature.
By R. W. Browne, M.A. London, 1884. 8vo.

———— A History of Roman Literature. By W.
S. Teuffel, translated by Wilhelm Wagner, Ph.D.
London, 1873. 2 vols. 8vo.

———— Bibliographical Clue to Latin Literature.
Edited after Dr. E. Hübner, with large additions by
the Rev. John E. B. Mayor. London, 1875. 12mo.

———— Guide to the Choice of Classical Books.
By Joseph B. Mayor. Third edition, with Supplementary List. London, 1885.

Manuscripts.—Guide to the Historian, the Bio-
grapher, the Antiquary, the man of literary curiosity,
and the collector of autographs, towards the verifica-
tion of Manuscripts, by reference to engraved fac-

similes of handwriting. [By Dawson Turner.] Yarmouth, 1848. Roy. 8vo. A most valuable alphabetical Index of the names of celebrated men, with references to the books where specimens of their writing can be found.

Mathematics. — Dictionnaire des Mathématiques appliqués. . . . Par H. Sonnet. Paris, 1867. Roy. 8vo.

Mechanics.—Knight's American Mechanical Dictionary . . . By Edward H. Knight. London and New York, 1874-77. 3 vols. royal 8vo.

———— Cyclopædia of Useful Arts, Mechanical and Chemical, Manufactures, Mining and Engineering. Edited by Charles Tomlinson. London, 1866. 3 vols. roy. 8vo.

Medical.—The Cyclopædia of Anatomy and Physiology. Edited by Robert B. Todd, M.D., F.R.S. London, 1835-59. 5 vols. in 6, royal 8vo.

———— A Dictionary of Practical Medicine . . . By James Copland. London, 1858. 3 vols. 8vo.

———— An Expository Lexicon of the terms, ancient and modern, in Medical and General Science ; including a complete Medico-Legal Vocabulary. . . By R. G. Mayne, M.D. London, 1860. 8vo.

———— Cooper's Dictionary of Practical Surgery and Encyclopædia of Surgical Science. New edition brought down to the present time by Samuel A. Lane. London, 1872. 2 vols. royal 8vo.

———— Medical Lexicon : a Dictionary of Medical

Science . . . by Robley Dunglison, M.D., LL.D.
A new edition enlarged and thoroughly revised by
Richard J. Dunglison, M.D.   Philadelphia, 1874.
Roy. 8vo.

Monograms. — Dictionnaire des Monogrammes,
marques figurées, lettres initiales, noms abrégés, etc.,
avec lesquels les Peintres, Dessinateurs, Graveurs et
Sculpteurs ont designé leurs noms.   Par François
Brulliot. Nouvelle édition.   Munich, 1832-34.   3
parts. Imp. 8vo.

Music.—General History of the Science and Practice
of Music. By Sir John Hawkins. London, 1776.
5 vols. 4to.

——— History of Music from the earliest ages to
the present period. By Charles Burney. London,
1776-89.   4 vols. 4to.

——— Biographie Universelle des Musiciens et
Bibliographie générale de la musique. Par F. J.
Fétis. Deuxième édition. Paris, 1860-65. 8 vols.
roy. 8vo.

——— Supplément et Complément, publiés sous la
direction de M. Arthur Pougin. Paris, 1878-80.
2 vols. roy. 8vo.

——— Dictionary of Music and Musicians.   Edited
by [Sir] G. Grove. London, 1878. 8vo. In progress.

Mythology.—Dictionary of Greek and Roman Biography and Mythology, edited by Dr. W. Smith.
1845-48. 3 vols. 8vo.

Natural History.—Dictionary of Natural History

Terms, with their derivations, including the various
orders, genera, and species. By David H. McNicoll,
M.D. London, 1863. Sm. 8vo.

Natural History.—See *Botany, Zoology.*

Painters.—A General Dictionary of Painters . . .
By Matthew Pilkington, A.M. A new edition, corrected and revised by R. A. Davenport. London,
1852. 8vo.

———— A Catalague Raisonné of the Works of the
most eminent Dutch, Flemish, and French Painters,
. . . to which is added a Brief Notice of the Scholars
and Imitators of the Great Masters of the above schools.
By John Smith. London, 1829–42. 9 parts. Roy. 8vo.

———— The Picture Collector's Manual, adapted
to the Professional Man and the Amateur ; being a
Dictionary of Painters . . . together with an alphabetical arrangement of the Scholars, Imitators, and
Copyists of the various masters, and a Classification
of Subjects. By James R. Hobbes. London, 1849.
2 vols. 8vo.

Peerage.—Courthope's "Historical Peerage,"founded
on Sir Nicholas Harris Nicolas's "Synopsis of the
Peerage," is an indispensable work, but it only refers
to English Titles. Mr. Solly's "Index of Hereditary
Titles of Honour" contains the Peerage and Baronet-
age of England, Scotland, and Ireland.

———— The Official Baronage of England, 1066 to
1885, by James E. Doyle (vols. 1–3. 4to.), has just
appeared.

Peerage.—Of the current peerages, Burke's, Dod's, Debrett's, and Foster's, all have their points of merit.

Periodicals.—Catalogue of Scientific Serials of all countries, including the Transactions of Learned Societies in the Natural, Physical and Mathematical Sciences, 1633–1876. By Samuel H. Scudder. Library of Harvard University, 1879. 8vo.—In this valuable list of periodicals, which is arranged geographically according to countries with an alphabet under each country, transactions and journals are joined together in the same arrangement. At the end there are an Index of Towns, an Index of Titles, and an Index of Minor Subjects.

——— An Index to Periodical Literature. By Wm. Fred. Poole. New York. Roy. 8vo. 1st ed. 1843 ; 2nd ed. 1848 ; 3rd ed. 1882.

——— Catalogue of Scientific Papers (1800–1863). Compiled and published by the Royal Society of London. London, 1867–72. 6 vols. 4to. (1864–73.) Vol. 7, 1877 ; Vol. 8, 1879.—Vol. 1, A-Clu ; Vol. 2, Coa-Gra ; Vol. 3, Gre-Lez ; Vol. 4, Lhe-Poz ; Vol. 5, Pra-Tiz ; Vol. 6, Tka-Zyl ; Vol. 7, A-Hyr ; Vol. 8, I-Zwi.

——— The celebrated Dr. Thomas Young published in the second volume of his *Course of Lectures on Natural Philosophy and the Mechanical Arts* (1807) a most valuable Catalogue of books and papers relating to the subject of his Lectures, which is classified minutely, and occupies 514 quarto pages in double

columns. In Kelland's new edition (1845) the
references are abridged and inserted after the several
lectures to which they refer.

Philology. — Max Müller's "Lectures on the
Science of Language"; Marsh's "Lectures" and
"Origin and History of the English Language";
Abp. Trench's "English, Past and Present";
"Select Glossary."

Physics.—Elementary Treatise on Natural Philosophy. By A. P. Deschanel. 8vo.

———— Elementary Treatise on Physics. By A.
Ganot, edited by E. Atkinson. Sm. 8vo.

Plate.—Old English Plate, ecclesiastical, decorative,
and domestic, its makers and marks. By Wilfred
Joseph Cripps, M.A., F.S.A. Second edition.
London, 1881. 8vo.

Plays.—See *Drama.*

Pottery.—Marks and Monograms on Pottery and
Porcelain of the Renaissance and Modern periods,
with historical notices of each Manufactory. . . . .
By William Chaffers. Fourth edition. London, 1874.
Roy. 8vo.

Prices.—History of Prices from 1793 to 1856. By
Thomas Tooke and William Newmarch. London,
1838-57. 6 vols. 8vo.

Prints.—An Introduction to the Study and Collection of Ancient Prints. By William Hughes
Willshire, M.D. Edin. Second edition, revised and
enlarged. London, 1877. 2 vols. 8vo.

Prints.—The Print Collector, an Introduction to the Knowledge necessary for forming a Collection of Ancient Prints. By J. Maberly, . . . Edited with Notes, an Account of Contemporary Etching and Etchers, and a Bibliography of Engraving. By Robert Hoe, jun. New York, 1880. Sq. 8vo.

———— Etching and Etchers. By P. G. Hamerton. New edition. London, 1876. 8vo.

Printing.—Typographia or the Printers' Instructor : including an Account of the Origin of Printing. . . . By J. Johnson, Printer. London, 1824. 2 vols. 8vo.

———— A Dictionary of the Art of Printing. By William Savage. London, 1841. 8vo.

Proverbs.—A Hand-Book of Proverbs, comprising an entire republication of Ray's Collection of English Proverbs . . . and a complete alphabetical Index . . . in which are introduced large additions collected by Henry G. Bohn, 1857. London, 1872.

———— A Polyglot of Foreign Proverbs, comprising French, Italian, German, Dutch, Spanish, Portuguese, and Danish, with English translations and a general Index. By Henry G. Bohn. London, 1867.

———— English Proverbs and Proverbial Phrases collected from the most authentic sources, alphabetically arranged and annotated. By W. Carew Hazlitt. London, 1869. 8vo. Second edition. London, 1882. Sm. 8vo.

Quotations.—Many Thoughts of Many Minds : being a Treasury of References, consisting of Selections from the Writings of the most celebrated Authors. Compiled and analytically arranged by Henry South-gate. Third edition. London, 1862. 8vo. Second Series. London, 1871. 8vo.

Quotations.—Noble Thoughts in Noble Language: a Collection of Wise and Virtuous Utterances in Prose and Verse, from the writings of the known good and the great unknown. Edited by Henry Southgate. London. 8vo.

—— Prose Quotations from Socrates to Macaulay, with Indexes. By S. Austin Allibone. Philadelphia, 1876. Roy. 8vo.

—— Poetical Quotations from Chaucer to Tennyson, with copious Indexes. By S. Austin Allibone. Philadelphia, 1875. Roy. 8vo.

—— A Dictionary of Quotations from the English Poets. By Henry G. Bohn. London, 1867. Sq. 8vo. Second edition. London. Sm. 8vo.

—— An Index to Familiar Quotations, selected principally from British Authors, with parallel passages from various writers, ancient and modern. By J. C. Grocott. Liverpool, 1863. Sm. 8vo.

—— Familiar Quotations: being an attempt to trace to their source passages and phrases in common use. By John Bartlett. Author's edition. London, Sm. 8vo.

—— Words, Facts and Phrases, a Dictionary of Curious, Quaint, and Out-of-the-Way Matters. By Eliezer Edwards. London, 1882. Sm. 8vo.

Quotations.—The Reader's Handbook of Allusions, References, Plots and Stories, with their appendices. By the Rev. E. Brewer, LL.D. . . Third edition. London, 1882. Sm. 8vo.

—— Dictionary of Phrase and Fable. . . By the Rev. E. Cobham Brewer, LL.D. Twelfth edition. London, no date.

—— A Dictionary of Latin and Greek Quotations, Proverbs, Maxims and Mottos, Classical and Mediæval, including Law Terms and Phrases. Edited by H. T. Riley, B.A. London, 1880. Sm. 8vo.

Receipts.—Cooley's Cyclopædia of Practical Receipts and Collateral Information in the Arts, Manufactures, Professions and Trades. . . designed as a comprehensive Supplement to the Pharmacopœia. . . Sixth edition, revised and greatly enlarged by Richard V. Tuson. London, 1880. 2 vols. 8vo.

Records.—Handbook of the Public Record Office. By F. S. Thomas, Secretary of the Public Record Office. London, 1853. Roy. 8vo.

—— Index to the Printed Reports of Sir Francis Palgrave, K.H., the Deputy-Keeper of the Public Records, 1840-1861. London, 1865. By John Edwards and Edward James Tabrum. In one alphabet.

Ritual.—Hierurgia ; or, Transubstantiation, Invocation of Saints, Relics and Purgatory, besides those other articles of Doctrine set forth in the Holy Sacrifice of the Mass expounded ; and the use of Holy

Water, Incense, and Images [etc.] Illustrated. By
D. Rock, D.D. Second edition. London, 1851. 8vo.

Ritual.—Hierurgia Anglicana ; or, Documents and
Extracts illustrative of the Ritual of the Church in
England after the Reformation. Edited by Members
of the Ecclesiological, late Cambridge Camden
Society. London, 1848. 8vo.

Sports.—An Encyclopædia of Rural Sports, or
complete account (historical, practical, and descriptive)
of Hunting, Shooting, Fishing, Racing, etc., etc.
By Delabere P. Blaine. A new edition. London,
1840. 8vo.

Taxes.—A Sketch of the History of Taxes in
England from the earliest times to the present day.
By Stephen Dowell. London, 1876. 8vo. Vol. 1
to the Civil War 1642.

Theology.—See *Ecclesiology.*

Topography. — A Topographical Dictionary of
England. . . By Samuel Lewis. Seventh edition.
London, 1849.

——— A Topographical Dictionary of Wales. . .
By Samuel Lewis. Fourth edition. London, 1849.
2 vols. 4to.

——— A Topographical Dictionary of Ireland.
. . . By Samuel Lewis. Second edition. London,
1842. 2 vols. 4to.

——— See *Geography.*

Wills.—An Index to Wills proved in the Court of
the Chancellor of the University of Oxford, and to

such of the records and other instruments and papers
of that Court as relate to matters or causes testa-
mentary. By the Rev. John Griffiths, M.A., Keeper
of the Archives. Oxford, 1862. Roy. 8vo. In one
alphabet, with a chronological list appended.

Zoology. — Nomenclator Zoologicus, continens
Nomina Systematica Generum Animalium tam viventium quam fossilium, secundum ordinem alphabeticum
disposita, adjectis auctoribus, libris in quibus reperi-
untur, anno editionis, etymologia et familiis, ad quas
pertinent, in singulis classibus. Auctore L. Agassiz.
. . . Soliduri, 1842-46. 4to.

———— Nomenclator Zoologicus, continens Nomina
Systematica generum animalium tam viventium quam
fossilium, secundum ordinem alphabeticum disposita
sub auspicis et sumptibus C. R. Societatis Zoologico-
Botanicæ conscriptus a Comite Augusto de Marschall
[1846-1868]. Vindobonæ, 1873. 8vo.

2. *Country.*

A library in a large country house should
contain a representative collection of English
literature, and also a selection of books of
reference from the previous list. Standard
Authors, in their best editions, County
Histories, Books of Travel, Books on Art,
and a representative collection of good

9

novels, will of course find a place upon
the shelves. A book such as Stevens's *My
English Library* will be a good guide to the
foundation of the library, but each collector
will have his special tastes, and he will need
guidance from the more particular bibliographies which are ready to his hand, and
a note of which will be found in Chapter V.
Room will also be found for sets of
Magazines, such as the *Gentleman's*, the
Edinburgh, and the *Quarterly*, and for the
Transactions of such Societies as the owner
may be member of. The issues of Publishing Societies form quite a library of themselves, and an account of these will be
found in Chapter VII.

We have seen on a previous page how
Napoleon wished to form a convenient
travelling library, in which everything
necessary could be presented in a com-
paratively small number of handy volumes.
Few men are like Napoleon in the wish
to carry such a library about with them;
but where space is scarce there are many
who find it necessary to exercise a wise

spirit of selection. This, however, each man must do for himself, as tastes differ so widely.

Auguste Comte succeeded in selecting a library in which all that it is necessary for a Positivist to know is included in 150 volumes, but this result is obtained by putting two or more books together to form one volume.

POSITIVIST LIBRARY FOR THE 19TH CENTURY
150 Volumes.

I. *Poetry.* (Thirty Volumes.)

The Iliad and the Odyssey, in 1 vol. without notes.

Æschylus, the King Œdipus of Sophocles, and Aristophanes, in 1 vol. without notes.

Pindar and Theocritus, with Daphnis and Chloe, in 1 vol. without notes.

Plautus and Terence, in 1 vol. without notes.

Virgil complete, Selections from Horace, and Lucan, in 1 vol. without notes.

Ovid, Tibullus, Juvenal, in 1 vol. without notes.

Fabliaux du Moyen Age, recueillies par Legrand D'Aussy.

Dante, Ariosto, Tasso, and Petrarch, in 1 vol. in Italian.

Select Plays of Metastasio and Alfieri, also in Italian.

I Promessi Sposi, by Manzoni, in 1 vol. in Italian.

Don Quixote, and the Exemplary Novels of Cervantes, in Spanish, in 1 vol.

Select Spanish Dramas, a collection edited by Don José Segundo Florez, in 1 vol. in Spanish.

The Romancero Espagnol, a selection, with the poem of the Cid, 1 vol. in Spanish.

Select Plays of P. Corneille.

Molière, complete.

Select Plays of Racine and Voltaire, in 1 vol.

La Fontaine's Fables, with some from Lamotte and Florian.

Gil Blas, by Lesage.

The Princess of Cleves, Paul and Virginia, and the Last of the Abencerrages, to be collected in 1 vol.

Les Martyres, par Chateaubriand.

Select Plays of Shakespeare.

Paradise Lost and Lyrical Poems of Milton.

Robinson Crusoe and the Vicar of Wakefield, in 1 vol.

Tom Jones, by Fielding, in English, or translated by Chéron.

The seven masterpieces of Walter Scott—Ivanhoe, Waverley, the Fair Maid of Perth, Quentin Durward, Woodstock (Les Puritains), the Heart of Midlothian, the Antiquary.

Select Works of Byron, Don Juan in particular to be suppressed.

Select Works of Goethe.

The Arabian Nights.

II. *Science.* (Thirty Volumes.)

Arithmetic of Condorcet, Algebra, and Geometry of Clairaut, the Trigonometry of Lacroix or Legendre, to form 1 vol.

Analytical Geometry of Auguste Comte, preceded by the Geometry of Descartes.

Statics, by Poinsot, with all his Memoirs on Mechanics.

Course of Analysis given by Navier at the Ecole Polytechnique, preceded by the Reflections on the Infinitesimal Calculus by Carnot.

Course of Mechanics given by Navier at the Ecole Polytechnique, followed by the Essay of Carnot on Equilibrum and Motion.

Theory of Functions, by Lagrange.

Popular Astronomy of Auguste Comte, followed by the Plurality of Worlds of Fontenelle.

Mechanical Physics of Fischer, translated and annotated by Biot.

Alphabetical Manual of Practical Philosophy, by John Carr.

The Chemistry of Lavoisier.

Chemical Statics, by Berthollet.

Elements of Chemistry, by James Graham.

Manual of Anatomy, by Meckel.

General Anatomy of Bichat, preceded by his Treatise on Life and Death.

The first volume of Blainville on the Organization of Animals.

Physiology of Richerand, with notes by Bérard.

Systematic Essay on Biology, by Segond, and his
    Treatise on General Anatomy.
Nouveaux Eléments de la Science de l'Homme, par
    Barthez (2nd edition, 1806).
La Philosophie Zoologique, par Lamarck.
Duméril's Natural History.
The Treatise of Guglielmini on the Nature of Rivers
    (in Italian).
Discourses on the Nature of Animals, by Buffon.
The Art of Prolonging Human Life, by Hufeland,
    preceded by Hippocrates on Air, Water, and
    Situation, and followed by Cornaro's book on
    a Sober and Temperate Life, to form 1 vol.
L'Histoire des Phlegmasies Chroniques, par Broussais,
    preceded by his Propositions de Médecine, and
    the Aphorisms of Hippocrates (in Latin), without
    commentary.
Les Eloges des Savans, par Fontenelle et Condorcet.

III. *History.* (Sixty Volumes.)

L'Abrégé de Géographie Universelle, par Malte Brun.
Geographical Dictionary of Rienzi.
Cook's Voyages, and those of Chardin.
History of the French Revolution, by Mignet.
Manual of Modern History, by Heeren.
Le Siècle de Louis XIV., par Voltaire.
Memoirs of Madame de Motteville.
The Political Testament of Richelieu, and the Life of
    Cromwell, to form 1 vol.

History of the Civil Wars of France, by Davila (in
    Italian).
Memoirs of Benvenuto Cellini (in Italian).
Memoirs of Commines.
L'Abrégé de l'Histoire de France, par Bossuet.
The Revolutions of Italy, by Denina.
The History of Spain, by Ascargorta.
History of Charles V., by Robertson.
History of England, by Hume.
Europe in the Middle Ages, by Hallam.
Ecclesiastical History, by Fleury.
Decline and Fall of the Roman Empire, by Gibbon.
Manual of Ancient History, by Heeren.
Tacitus (Complete), the Translation of Dureau de la
    Malle.
Herodotus and Thucydides, in 1 vol.
Plutarch's Lives, translation of Dacier.
Cæsar's Commentaries, and Arrian's Alexander, in
    1 vol.
Voyage of Anacharsis, by Barthelemy.
History of Art among the Ancients, by Winckelmann.
Treatise on Painting, by Leonardo da Vinci (in
    Italian).
Memoirs on Music, by Grétry.

IV. *Synthesis.* (Thirty Volumes.)

Aristotle's Politics and Ethics, in 1 vol.
The Bible.
The Koran.

The City of God, by St. Augustine.

The Confessions of St. Augustine, followed by St. Bernard on the Love of God.

The Imitation of Jesus Christ, the original, and the translation into verse, by Corneille.

The Catechism of Montpellier, preceded by the Exposition of Catholic Doctrine, by Bossuet, and followed by St. Augustine's Commentary on the Sermon on the Mount.

L'Histoire des Variations Protestantes, par Bossuet.

Discourse on Method, by Descartes, preceded by the Novum Organum of Bacon, and followed by the Interpretation of Nature, by Diderot.

Selected Thoughts of Cicero, Epictetus, Marcus Aurelius, Pascal, and Vauvenargues, followed by Conseils d'une Mère, by Madame de Lambert, and Considérations sur les Mœurs, par Duclos.

Discourse on Universal History, by Bossuet, followed by the Esquisse Historique, by Condorcet.

Treatise on the Pope, by De Maistre, preceded by the Politique Sacrée, by Bousset.

Hume's Philosophical Essays, preceded by the two Dissertations on the Deaf, and the Blind, by Diderot, and followed by Adam Smith's Essay on the History of Astronomy.

Theory of the Beautiful, by Barthez, preceded by the Essay on the Beautiful, by Diderot.

Les Rapports du Physique et du Moral de l'Homme, par Cabanis.

Treatise on the Functions of the Brain, by Gall,
    preceded by Letters on Animals, by Georges
    Leroy.
Le Traité sur l'Irritation et la Folie, par Broussais
    (first edition).
The Positive Philosophy of Auguste Comte (con-
    densed by Miss Martineau), his Positive Politics,
    his Positivist Catechism, and his Subjective
    Synthesis.

Paris, 3 Dante 66 (Tuesday, 18th July, 1854).
AUGUSTE COMTE,
(10 rue Monsieur le Prince).

This is an interesting list as having been
compiled with special thought by a celebrated man, but in many of its details it
is little likely to find acceptance with the
general reader. It seems rather odd to an
Englishman to find the *Princess of Cleves*
included, while Shakespeare is only to be
found in a selection of his plays. It is not
Comte's fault that science has not stood
still since 1854, and that his selection of
books is rather out of date.

A list of a hundred good novels is likely
to be useful to many, but few lists would be

open to more criticism, for readers differ
more as to what constitutes a good novel
than upon any other branch of literature.
The following list was contributed by Mr.
F. B. Perkins to the *Library Journal* (vol. i.
p. 166). The titles are very short, and they
are put down in no particular order. Most
of us will miss some favourite book, but
two people, Mr. Perkins says, have agreed
on this list within four or five items. He
says he was tempted to add a few alterna-
tives, as Amadis de Gaul, Morte d'Arthur,
Paul and Virginia, Frankenstein, Rasselas,
etc.

Don Quixote.	Minister's Wooing.
Gil Blas.	Undine.
Pilgrim's Progress.	Sintram.
Tale of a Tub.	Thisdolf.
Gulliver.	Peter Schlemihl.
Vicar of Wakefield.	Sense and Sensibility.
Robinson Crusoe.	Pride and Prejudice.
Arabian Nights.	Anastasius.
Decameron.	Amber Witch.
Wilhelm Meister.	Mary Powell.
Vathek.	Household of Sir T. More.
Corinne.	Cruise of the Midge.

Guy Mannering.	Tom Cringle's Lodge.
Antiquary.	Japhet in Search of a Father.
Bride of Lammermoor.	Peter Simple.
Legend of Montrose.	Midshipman Easy.
Rob Roy.	Scarlet Letter.
Woodstock.	House with the Seven Gables
Ivanhoe.	Wandering Jew.
Talisman.	Mysteries of Paris.
Fortunes of Nigel.	Humphry Clinker.
Old Mortality.	Eugénie Grandet.
Quentin Durward.	Knickerbocker's New York.
Heart of Midlothian.	Charles O'Malley.
Kenilworth.	Harry Lorrequer.
Fair Maid of Perth.	Handy Andy.
Vanity Fair.	Elsie Venner.
Pendennis.	Challenge of Barletta.
Newcomes.	Betrothed (Manzoni's).
Esmond.	Jane Eyre.
Adam Bede.	Counterparts.
Mill on the Floss.	Charles Anchester.
Romola.	Tom Brown's Schooldays.
Middlemarch.	Tom Brown at Oxford.
Pickwick.	Lady Lee's Widowhood.
Chuzzlewit.	Horseshoe Robinson.
Nickleby.	Pilot.
Copperfield.	Spy.
Tale of Two Cities.	Last of the Mohicans.
Dombey.	My Novel.
Oliver Twist.	On the Heights.

Bleak House.   Woman in White.
Tom Jones.   Love me little love me long.
Three Guardsmen.   Two Years Ago.
Monte Cristo.   Yeast.
Les Miserables.   Coningsby.
Notre Dame.   Young Duke.
Consuelo.   Hyperion.
Fadette (Fanchon).   Kavanagh.
Uncle Tom's Cabin.   Bachelor of the Albany.

CHAPTER V.

GENERAL BIBLIOGRAPHIES.

 GOOD collection of bibliographies is indispensable for a public library, and will also be of great use in a private library when its possessor is a true lover of books. One of the most valuable catalogues of this class of books is the " Hand-List of Bibliographies, Classified Catalogues, and Indexes placed in the Reading Room of the British Museum for Reference" (1881). It is not intended to give in this chapter anything like a complete account of these books, as a separate volume would be required to do justice to them. Here it will be sufficient to indicate some of the foremost works in the class. The catalogues of some of our chief libraries are

amongst the most valuable of bibliographies
for reference. The Catalogue of the Library
of the London Institution is one of the hand-
somest ever produced.[1]   Unfortunately the
cost of production was too great for the
funds of the Institution, and the elaborate
Catalogue of Tracts was discontinued after
the letter F.

The London Library being a specially
well-selected one, the catalogue (which is a
good example of a short-titled catalogue) is
particularly useful for ready reference.[2]

The Royal Institution Library is very rich

[1] A Catalogue of the Library of the London Institution, systematically classed. [London] 1835. 5 vols.
royal 8vo.   Vol. 1 (1835), General Library; vol. 2
(1840), Tracts and Pamphlets arranged in alphabetical
order as far as the letter F. (never completed); vol. 3
(1843), General Library, Additions; vol. 4 (1852),
Additions from 1843 to 1852.

[2] Catalogue of the London Library, 12, St. James's
Square, S.W.   With Preface, Laws and Regulations,
List of Members and Classified Index of Subjects.
By Robert Harrison.   Fourth edition.   Sold at the
Library, 1875, royal 8vo. pp. 1022.

——— Supplemental Volume, 1875–1880, sold at
the Library, 1881, royal 8vo. pp. 219.

in British Topography, and the catalogue forms a convenient handbook.[1]

The Catalogue of the Patent Office Library is by no means a model, but the second volume forms a good book of reference.[2] Many other catalogues might be mentioned, but these will be sufficient for our present purpose. There is great want of a good Handbook of Literature, with the prices of the different books. Until this want is supplied good booksellers' catalogues will be found the most trustworthy guides. Pre-eminent among these are the catalogues of

[1] A New Classified Catalogue of the Library of the Royal Institution of Great Britain with Indexes of Authors and Subjects, and a list of Historical Pamphlets, Chronologically arranged. By Benjamin Vincent. London. Sold at the Royal Institution. 1857, 8vo. pp. xvii.-928.

———— Vol. II., including the Additions from 1857 to 1882. London. Sold at the Royal Institution. 1882. 8vo. pp. xvii.–388.

[2] Catalogue of the Library of the Patent Office, arranged alphabetically. In two volumes : vol. 1, Authors ; vol. 2, Subjects. London. Published and Sold at the Commissioners of Patents Sale Department. 1881–83. Royal 8vo.

Mr. Quaritch, and the "Catalogue of upwards of fifty thousand volumes of ancient and modern books," published by Messrs. Willis and Sotheran in 1862. Mr. Quaritch's catalogues are classified with an index of subjects and authors.[1] A previous General Catalogue was issued in 1874, and a Supplement 1875–77 (pp. iv. 1672). Now Mr. Quaritch is issuing in sections a new Catalogue on a still larger scale, which is of the greatest value.

For the study of early printed books, Hain,[2] Panzer,[3] and Maittaire's[4] books are indispensable.

[1] A General Catalogue of Books, offered for sale to the public at the affixed prices. By Bernard Quaritch London, 15, Piccadilly, 1880. 8vo. pp. x.–2395.

[2] 1457–1500. HAIN (L.). Repertorium Bibliographicum in quo libri omnes ab arte typographica inventa usque ad annum MD typis expressi, ordine alphabetico vel simpliciter enumerantur vel adcuratius recensentur. Stuttgartiæ, 1826–38. 2 vols. 8vo.

[3] 1457–1536. PANZER (G. W.). Annales Typographici ab artis inventæ origine ad annum 1536. Norimbergæ, 1793–1803. 11 vols. 4to.

[4] 1457–1664. MAITTAIRE (M.). Annales Typographici ab artis inventæ origine ad annum 1664, cum

For general literature Brunet's Manual[1] stands pre-eminent in its popularity. It has held its own since 1810, when it was first published in three volumes, demy octavo. Graesse's Trésor[2] is less known out of Germany, but it also is a work of very great value. Ebert's work[3] is somewhat out of date now, but it still has its use. Watt's Bibliotheca[4] is one of the most valuable bibliographies ever published, chiefly on

Supplemento Michaelis Denisii. Hag. Com.et Viennæ, 1719–89. 7 vols in 11 parts.

[1] BRUNET (J. C.). Manuel du Libraire, cinquième édition. Paris, 1860-65. 6 vols. 8vo. Supplément par P. Deschamps et G. Brunet. Paris, 1878-80, 2 vols. Royal 8vo.

[2] GRAESSE (J. G. T.). Trésor de Livres rares et précieux ou Nouveau Dictionnaire Bibliographique. Dresde, 1859-69. 7 vols. 4to.

[3] EBERT (F. A.). Allgemeines bibliographisches Lexikon. Leipzig, 1821-30. 2 vols. 4to.

——— A General Bibliographical Dictionary, from the German [by A. Brown]. Oxford, 1837. 4 vols. 8vo.

[4] WATT (R.). Bibliotheca Britannica : a General Index to British and Foreign Literature. In two parts, Authors and Subjects. Edinburgh, 1824. 4 vols. 4to.

account of the index of subjects which
gives information that cannot be found elsewhere. The titles were largely taken from
second-hand sources, and are in many
instances marred by misprints. Every one
who uses it must wish that it was brought
down to date, but it is scarcely likely that
any one will sacrifice a life to such labour as
would be necessary. Moreover, the popular
feeling is somewhat adverse to universal
bibliographies, and it is thought that the
literature of his own country is sufficiently
large a subject for the bibliographer to
devote his time to.

English literature has not been neglected
by English bibliographers, although a full
bibliography of our authors is still a crying
want. Complete lists of the works of some
of our greatest authors have still to be made,
and it is to be hoped that all those who have
the cause of bibliography at heart will join
to remedy the great evil. It would be quite
possible to compile a really national work by
a system of co-operation such as was found
workable in the case of the Philological

Society's Dictionary of the English Language. Sub-editors of the different letters might be appointed, and to them all titles could be sent. When the question of printing arose, it would be well to commence with the chief authors. These bibliographies might be circulated, by which means many additions would be made to them, and then they could be incorporated in the general alphabet. In such a bibliography books in manuscript ought to be included, as well as printed books. Although there is little doubt that many books still remain unregistered, we are well supplied with catalogues of books made for trade purposes. Maunsell[1] was the first to publish such a list, and in 1631 was published a catalogue of books issued between 1626 and 1631.[2]

---

[1] Before 1595. MAUNSELL (A.). Catalogue of English printed Books. London, 1595. 4to. Part 1, Divinitie. Part 2, Sciences Mathematicall.

[2] 1626–1631. A Catalogue of certaine Bookes which have been published and (by authoritie) printed in England both in Latine and English, since the year 1626 until November, 1631. London, 1631. 4to.

William London[1] published his Catalogue in 1658, and Clavell's his in 1696.[2] Bent's Catalogue, published in 1786, went back to 1700,[3] and this was continued annually as the London Catalogue. The British and

[1] Before 1658. LONDON (WILLIAM). A Catalogue of the most vendible Books in England, orderly and alphabetically digested. With a Supplement. 1658-60. 4to.

[2] 1666-1695. CLAVELL (R.). General Catalogue of Books printed in England since the dreadful Fire of London, 1666. Fourth edition. London, 1696. Folio.

[3] 1700-1786. A General Catalogue of Books in all Languages, Arts, and Sciences, printed in Great Britain and published in London. London (W. Bent), 1786. 8vo.

1811. London Catalogue of Books. London (W. Bent), 1811. 8vo.

1810-1831. London Catalogue of Books. London (W. Bent), 1831. 8vo.

1816-1851. London Catalogue of Books. London (Hodgson), 1851. 8vo. Classified Index. London (Hodgson), 1853.

1831-1855. London Catalogue of Books. London (Hodgson), 1855.

English Catalogues[1] followed, and the latter is also published annually.[2]

For early printed books, Ames and Herbert's great work[3] is of much value, but information respecting our old literature has increased so much of late that a new history of typographical antiquities is sadly needed. Mr. Blades has done the necessary work for Caxton, but the first English printer's successors require similar treatment.

William Thomas Lowndes, the son of

---

[1] 1837–52. The British Catalogue. Sampson Low, 1853. And Index. 2 vols. 8vo.

[2] 1835–1880. The English Catalogue of Books. Sampson Low. And Indexes. 8vo. *Continued annually.*

[3] 1471–1600. AMES (JOSEPH). Typographical Antiquities : being an Historical Account of Printing in England, with some Memoirs of our Antient Printers, and a Register of the Books printed by them . . . with an Appendix concerning Printing in Scotland, Ireland to the same time. London, 1749. 4to. 1 vol. Considerably augmented by W. Herbert. London, 1785–90. 3 vols. 4to. Enlarged by T. F. Dibdin. London, 1810–19. 4 vols. 4to.

an eminent bookseller and publisher, and
himself a bookseller, published in 1834
his *Bibliographer's Manual*,[1] which has remained the great authority for English
Literature. It had become very scarce
when Henry Bohn, in 1857, brought out
a new edition with additions in a series
of handy volumes, which is an indispensable book of reference, although it is
far from being the complete work that is
required.

Allibone's *Dictionary*[2] contains much that
is omitted in Lowndes's *Manual*, but it
is more literary than bibliographical in
its scope. The well-selected criticisms
appended to the titles of the several
books are of considerable interest and
value to the reader. Mr. W. C. Hazlitt's

---

[1] LOWNDES (W. T.). The Bibliographer's Manual
of English Literature. London, 1834. 4 vols. 8vo.
New Edition, by H. G. Bohn. London, 1857–64.
6 vols. Sm. 8vo.

[2] ALLIBONE (S. A.). Dictionary of English Literature, and British and American Authors. Philadelphia,
1859--71. 3 vols. Royal 8vo.

Handbooks[1] are exceedingly valuable as containing information respecting a class of books which has been much neglected in bibliographical works. The compiler has been indefatigable for some years past in registering the titles of rare books as they occurred at public sales.

Mr. Collier's account of rare books,[2] founded on his Bridgewater Catalogue (1837), is of great use for information respecting out-of-the-way literature, as also is Mr. Corser's descriptive Catalogue of Old English Poetry.[3]

---

[1] HAZLITT (W. CAREW). Handbook to the Popular, Poetical, and Dramatic Literature of Great Britain, from the Invention of Printing to the Restoration. London (J. Russell Smith), 1867. 8vo.
——— Collections and Notes, 1867–1876. London (Reeves & Turner), 1876. 8vo.
——— Second Series of Bibliographical Collections and Notes on Early English Literature, 1474–1700. London (Bernard Quaritch), 1882.
[2] COLLIER (J. P.). A Bibliographical and Critical Account of the rarest books in the English language, alphabetically arranged. London, 1865. 2 vols. 8vo.
[3] CORSER (T.). Collectanea Anglo-Poetica ; or a

Accounts of books published in Gaelic,[1] in Welsh,[2] and in Irish,[3] have been published. The works of American authors are included in Allibone's *Dictionary*, referred to under English literature, but special books have also been prepared, such as Trübner's Guide,[4] Stevens's American Books in the British

bibliographical and descriptive Catalogue of a portion of a Collection of Early English Poetry. Manchester (Chetham Society), 1860-79. 9 vols. Sm. 4to.

[1] *Gaelic.* Bibliotheca Scoto-Celtica ; or, an account of all the books which have been published in the Gaelic Language. By John Reid. Glasgow, 1832. 8vo.

[2] *Welsh.* Cambrian Bibliography : containing an account of the books printed in the Welsh Language ; or relating to Wales, from the year 1546 to the end of the 18th century. By W. Rowlands. Llanidloes, 1869. 8vo.

[3] *Irish.* Transactions of the Iberno-Celtic Society for 1820. Containing a chronological account of nearly four hundred Irish writers . . . carried down to the year 1750, with a descriptive Catalogue of such of their works as are still extant. By E. O'Reilly. Dublin, 1820. 4to.

[4] Trübner's Bibliographical Guide to American Literature : a classed list of books published in the United States of America during the last forty years. London, 1859. 8vo.

Museum,[1] and Leypoldt's great book, the American Catalogue.[2] Catalogues of Books on America, such as those of Obadiah Rich, have also been compiled, but these are more properly special bibliographies. France has always stood in a foremost position in respect to bibliography, and she alone has a national work on her literature, which stands in the very first rank—this is due to the enthusiastic bibliographer Querard.[3] A better model as to what a national

---

[1] Catalogue of the American Books in the Library of the British Museum. Christmas, 1856. By H. Stevens. London, 1866. 8vo.

[2] The American Catalogue under the direction of F. Leypoldt. New York, 1880. 2 vols. 4to. Suppl. 1876–84. Compiled under the editorial direction of R. R. Bowker by Miss Appleton. New York, 1885.

[3] QUERARD (J. M.). La France Littéraire, ou Dictionnaire Bibliographique des Savants qui ont écrit en français, plus particulièrement pendant les XVIIIe et XIXe siècles. Paris, 1827–64. 12 vols. 8vo.

———— Littérature Française contemporaine (1826–49). Continuation de la France Littéraire. Paris, 1842–57. 6 vols. 8vo.

bibliography should be could not well be found. The catalogue of current literature, which bears the name of O. Lorenz, is also an excellent work.[1]

German literature has been, and is, well registered. Heyse,[2] Maltzahn,[3] Heinsius,[4] and Kayser,[5] have all produced valuable

---

[1] LORENZ (O.). Catalogue de la Librairie Française 1840–1865. 4 vols. 1866–1875. 2 vols. 8vo. The Catalogue of Books from 1876 to 1885 is in preparation.
——— Tables des Matières, 1840–1875. Paris, 1879-80. 2 vols. 8vo.

[2] [HEYSE (C. W.).] Bücherschatz der deutschen National-Litteratur des XVI und XVII Jahrhunderts. Systematisch geordnetes Verzeichniss einer reichhaltigen Sammlung deutschen Büchen. Berlin, 1854. 8vo.

[3] MALTZAHN (W. VON). Deutschen Bücherschatz des sechszehnten, siebenzehnten und achtzehnten bis um die Mitte des neunzehnten Jahrhunderts. Jena, 1875. 8vo.

[4] HEINSIUS (W.). Allgemeines Bücher Lexicon, 1700–1815 Leipzig, 1812-56. 14 vols. 4to. 7th Supplement.

[5] KAYSER (C. G.). Index Librorum. Vollständiges Bücher-Lexicon, enthaltend alle von 1750 bis zu Ende des Jahres (–1876) in Deutschland . . . gedruckten Bücher. Leipzig, 1834-77. 4to.

works. Heinsius published his original Lexicon in 1812, and Kayser his in 1834, and Supplements to both of these have been published about every ten years. A more condensed work was commenced by A. Kirchhoff in 1856, containing the catalogue of works published from 1851 to 1855; a second volume of the next five years appeared in 1861, and since Kirchhoff's death Hinrichs has published a volume every five years. The Leipzig Book-fairs have had their catalogues ever since 1594, and the half-yearly volumes now bearing the name of Hinrichs,[1] which have been published regularly since 1798, and to which the Fair catalogues succumbed in 1855, may be considered as their legitimate successors.

The Literature of Holland is well recorded

[1] HINRICHS (J. C.). Verzeichniss der Bücher . . . welche in Deutschland vom Januar, 1877, bis zum (December, 1885) neu erschienen oder neu aufgelegt worden sind. Leipzig, 1876–80. 12mo. *In progress.*
———— Repertorium über die nach den . . . Verzeichnissen, 1871–75, erschienenen Bücher. Von E. Baldamus. (1876–80.) Leipzig, 1877–82. 12mo.

by Campbell[1] and Abkoude,[2] and for Belgium
there is the *Bibliographie de Belgique.*[3]　Italy
can boast of a Gamba[4] and a Bertocci,[5] and

[1] CAMPBELL (M.F.A.G.).　Annales de la Typo-
graphie Néerlandaise au XVᵉ Siècle.　La Haye, 1874.
8vo.

────── 1ᵉʳ Supplément.　La Haye, 1878.　8vo.

[2] ABKOUDE (J. VAN).　Naamregister van de be-
kendste . . . Nederduitsche Boeken . . . 1600 tot 1761.
Nu overzien en tot het jaar 1787 vermeerderd door
R. Arrenberg.　Rotterdam, 1788.　4to.

────── Alphabetische Naamlijst van Boeken 1790
tot 1832, Amsterdam, 1835.　4to.　1833–1875.　Amsterdam, 1858–78.　3 vols.　4to.

────── Wetenschappelijk Register behoorende bij
Brinkman's Alphabetische Naamlijsten van Boeken
. . . 1850–75 . . . bewerkt door R. van der Meulen.
Amsterdam, 1878.　4to.

[3] Bibliographie de Belgique.　Journal Officiel de
la Librairie.　Année 1.　Bruxelles, 1876.　8vo.

[4] GAMBA (B.).　Serie dei testi di Lingua Italiana
e di altri opere importanti nella Italiana letteratura
del Secolo XV al XIX.　Quarta edizione.　Venezia,
1839.　8vo.

[5] BERTOCCI (D. G.).　Repertorio bibliografico delle
opere stampate in Italia nel Secolo XIX.　Vol. I.
Roma, 1876.　8vo.

a public office publishes the *Bibliografia Italiana.*[1]

Spain is fortunate in possessing a splendid piece of bibliography in the great works of Antonio.[2] Some years ago, when I was occupied in cataloguing one of the chief collections of Spanish books in this country, I was in the daily habit of consulting these *Bibliothecas,* and while comparing the books themselves with the printed titles, I seldom found a mistake. Hidalgo's[3] work and the Boletin[4] show that at the present time

[1] Bibliografia Italiana: Giornale compilato sui documenti communicati dal Ministero dell' Istruzione Pubblica. Anno 1-14. 1867-80. Firenze, 1868-81. 8vo. In progress.

[2] ANTONIO (N.). Bibliotheca Hispana Vetus sive Hispani Scriptores . . . ad annum Christi 1500 floruerunt. Matriti, 1788. 2 vols. Folia.

—— Bibliotheca Hispana Nova sive Hispanorum Scriptorum qui ab anno 1500 ad 1684 floruere notitia. Matriti, 1783-1788. 2 vols. Folio.

[3] HIDALGO (D.). Diccionario general de Bibliografia Española. Madrid, 1862-79. 6 vols. 8vo.

[4] Boletin de la Libreria. Año 1. 1873. Madrid, 1874. 8vo. In progress.

bibliography is not neglected in that country.

The works of Barbosa Machado [1] and Silva [2] show that Portugal is not behind the sister kingdom in the love for bibliography.

Bibliographies of other countries might be mentioned here, but space will not permit. There is one branch of general bibliography to which special attention has been paid for a long period of years. O. Placcius published his *Theatrum Anonymorum et Pseudonymorum* at Hamburgh in 1674 (2nd ed. 1708). Villani continued the record of pseudonymous literature by publishing at Parma, in 1689, a small volume entitled *La Visiera alzata.* J. C. Mylius published his *Bibliotheca Anonymorum et Pseudonymorum* at Hamburgh in 1740.

---

[1] BARBOSA MACHADO (D.). Bibliotheca Lusitana, historica, critica e cronologica. Na qual se comprehende a noticia dos authores Portuguezes, e das obras que compuserão. Lisboa, 1741–59. 4 vols. Folio.

[2] SILVA (J. F. DA). Diccionario bibliographico Portuguez. Lisboa, 1858–70. Tom. 1–9. 8vo.

Barbier's great work on the Anonymous in French Literature was first published in 1806–8, the second edition appeared in 1822–27, and the third in 1872–78, as a continuation to the second edition of Querard's *Les Supercheries Littéraires*. Querard's work is more curious than useful, because the author has entered into minute questions of authorship which do not really belong to the domain of bibliography. Manne's volume (1834) is not of much value. Lancetti published an octavo volume on Pseudonyms in Italian (1836), but Barbier's work was not worthily imitated in any other country until Mr. Paterson commenced the publication of the very valuable work of the late Mr. Halkett.[1]

[1] A Dictionary of the Anonymous and Pseudonymous Literature of Great Britain, including the works of Foreigners written in or translated into the English Language. By the late Samuel Halkett, and the late Rev. John Laing. Edinburgh (William Paterson), 1882–85. Vols. 1, 2, 3 (to 'Tis).

CHAPTER VI.

IBLIOGRAPHIES of special subjects are more useful than any other books in the formation of a library. The articles in the new edition of the *Encyclopædia Britannica* will be found valuable for this purpose, but those who wish for fuller information must refer to Dr. Julius Petzholdt's elaborate *Bibliotheca Bibliographica* (Leipzig, 1866), or to the *Bibliographie des Bibliographies* of M. Léon Vallée (Paris, 1885). The late Mr. Cornelius Walford contributed a paper "On Special Collections of Books" to the Transactions of the Conference of Librarians, 1877 (pp. 45–49), in which he specially referred to the subject of Insurance.

In the present chapter I propose to refer to some of the most useful bibliographies, but to save space the full titles will not be given, and this is the less necessary as they can mostly be found in the above books or in that useful little volume we owe to the authorities of the British Museum —" Hand-list of Bibliographies, Classified Catalogues, and Indexes placed in the Reading-room," 1881.

Agriculture.—Weston's Tracts on Practical Agriculture and Gardening (1773), contains a Chronological Catalogue of English Authors, and Donaldson's Agricultural Biography (1854) brings the subject down to a later date. Victor Donatien de Musset-Pathay published a *Bibliographie Agronomique* in 1810, and Loudon's *Encyclopædia of Agriculture* contains the Literature and Bibliography of Agriculture, British, French, German, and American.

Ana.—In Peignot's *Repertoire de Bibliographies Spéciales* (1810) will be found at pp. 211–268, a list of books of Ana, and Gabriel Antoine Joseph Hécart published at Valenciennes, 1821, under the name of J. G. Phitakaer, a bibliography entitled "Anagrapheana." Namur's *Bibliographie des Ouvrages publiés sous le nom d'Ana* was published at Bruxelles in 1839. The late Sir William Stirling Maxwell

made a collection of books of Ana, a privately printed
catalogue of which he issued in 1860.

Angling.—Sir Henry Ellis printed privately in 1811
a small octavo pamphlet of 21 pages which he entitled
"A Catalogue of Books on Angling, with some brief
notices of several of their authors," which was an
extract from the *British Bibliographer.* In 1836,
Pickering printed a *Bibliotheca Piscatoria,* which was
formed upon Sir Henry Ellis's corrected copy of the
above Catalogue. Mr. J. Russell Smith published in
1856 "A Bibliographical Catalogue of English writers
on Angling and Ichthyology," which was soon super-
ceded by the following work by Mr. T. Westwood.
" A new Bibliotheca Piscatoria, or a general Catalogue
of Angling and Fishing Literature." London, 1861
(another edition, edited conjointly with T. Satchell,
1883). Mr. R. Blakey published in 1855, "Angling
Literature of all Nations." London, 1855. 12mo.
Mr. J. J. Manley, M.A., published in 1883,
" Literature of Sea and River Fishing," as one of the
Handbooks of the International Fisheries Exhibition.

Architecture.—LACROIX (E.). Bibliographie des
Ingénieurs, des Architectes, des Chefs d'Usines
industrielles, des Elèves des Ecoles polytechniques
et professionnelles et des Agriculteurs. Première
(—Troisième) Série. Paris, 1864-67. 4to.

Assurance (Life).—Lewis Pocock published "A
Chronological List of Books and Single Papers"
relating to this subject in 1836, a second edition of
which was published in 1842.

Astronomy.—Lalande published his valuable "Bibliographie Astronomique" at Paris, 1803. Otto Struve's Catalogue of the Library of the Pulkova Observatory, published at St. Petersburg in 1860, is highly esteemed by astronomers. The first part of the Catalogue of the United States Naval Observatory at Washington, by Prof. E. S. Holden, is devoted to Astronomical Bibliography.

—— HOUZEAU (J. C.) and LANCASTER (A.). Bibliographie générale de l'Astronomie. Bruxelles, 1880. 8vo. In progress.

—— Mr. E. B. Knobel, Secretary of the Royal Astronomical Society, printed in the *Monthly Notices* of that Society for November, 1876 (pp. 365-392), a very useful short Reference Catalogue of Astronomical Papers and Researches, referring more especially to (1) Double Stars; (2) Variable Stars; (3) Red Stars; (4) Nebulæ and Clusters; (5) Proper Motions of Stars; (6) Parallax and Distance of Stars; (7) Star Spectra. Mr. E. S. Holden's "Index Catalogue of Books and Memoirs relating to Nebulæ and Clusters of Stars" was printed in the *Smithsonian Miscellaneous Collections* in 1877.

Bible.—The famous Le Long published at Paris, in 1713, his "Discours historiques sur les principales éditions des Bibles polyglottes," and in 1723, in two volumes, folio, his great work "Bibliotheca Sacra." This was edited and continued by A. G. Masch, and published at Halæ Magd. in five volumes, quarto.

1774-97.   T. Llewelyn published in 1768 " Historical
Account of the British or Welsh Versions and editions
of the Bible."   A privately printed "List of various
editions of the Bible" was issued in 1778, which has been
attributed to Dr. Ducarel.   John Lewis's "Complete
History of the several Translations of the Holy Bible
and New Testament into English" was published
in 1818, and Dr. Henry Cotton's "List of Editions"
(Oxford, 1821, 2nd edition, 1852) was intended as
an Appendix to that work.   Orme's *Bibliotheca
Biblica* was published at Edinburgh in 1824, and
Hartwell Horne's *Manual of Biblical Bibliography*
at London in 1839.   Bagster's *Bible in Every Land*
(1848), although not strictly bibliographical, must
be mentioned here, because it gives under each
language a notice of all versions published in that
language.   Lowndes' British Librarian or Book Col-
lector's Guide.   Class I.   Religion and its History.
London, 1839.   8vo.   Parts 1, 2, 3 are devoted to
Holy Scriptures, Biblical Commentaries, Biblical
Disquisitions, Scripture Biography, Scripture Geo-
graphy, etc.   The work itself was left incomplete.
Dr. H. Cotton published at Oxford, in 1855,
a work entitled "Rhemes and Doway.   An
Attempt to show what has been done by Roman
Catholics for the diffusion of the Holy Scriptures in
English."   In 1859 J. G. Shea published at New
York a "Bibliographical Account of Catholic Bibles,
Testaments, and other portions of Scripture translated

from the Latin Vulgate, and printed in the United
States," and in 1861 E. B. O'Callaghan published at
Albany a "List of editions of the Holy Scriptures
and parts thereof, printed in America previous to
1860." E. Reuss published at Brunswick, in 1872,
a Bibliography of the Greek New Testament. Dr.
Isaac Hall printed a Critical Bibliography of
American Greek Testaments at Philadelphia in
1883. Mr. Henry Stevens, the eminent bibliographer, is a special authority on Bibles, and his
work, entitled "The Bibles in the Caxton Exhibition,
1877, or a bibliographical description of nearly one
thousand representative Bibles in various languages,
chronologically arranged" (London, 1878), contains
some of the information he possesses.

Biography.—Oettinger's *Bibliographie Biographique
Universelle* (1854) is a most useful work, although it
is now unfortunately somewhat out of date.

Book-keeping.—B. F. Foster's *Origin and Progress
of Book-keeping* (1852) contains an account of books
published on this subject from 1543 to 1852.

Botany.—Pritzel's *Thesaurus Literaturæ Botanicæ*
(1851, another edition 1872-77) is *the* Bibliography of
the subject, and this work is supplemented by Mr.
Daydon Jackson's Index of Botany, published by the
Index Society. Trimen's Botanical Bibliography of
the British counties, London, 1874. 8vo.

Chemistry.—R. Ruprecht, Bibliotheca Chemica et
Pharmaceutica, 1858-70. *Göttingen*, 1872.

Classics.—Dr. Edward Harwood published his "View of the various editions of the Greek and Roman Classics" in 1790. He was followed in 1802 by Thomas Frognall Dibdin, whose work was much enlarged, and reappeared in several editions; the fourth and best being published in 1827 (2 vols. 8vo.). J. W. Moss published his "Manual of Classical Bibliography" in 1825, 2 vols. 8vo. Henry G. Bohn's General Catalogue, Part II. Section I. 1850, contains a valuable list of Greek and Latin Classics. Engelmann's Bibliotheca Scriptorum Classicorum et Græcorum et Latinorum (1858) is an elaborate work on the subject, and Professor John E. B. Mayor's translation and adaptation of Dr. Hübner's Bibliographical Clue to Latin Literature will be found to be a very useful handbook.

Commerce.—See *Trade.*

Dialects.—Mr. J. Russell Smith published, in 1839, a useful "Bibliographical List of the Works that have been published towards illustrating the Provincial Dialects of England" (24 pages). When the Rev. Professor Skeat started the English Dialect Society, he at once laid the foundation of an extensive Bibliographical List to include MSS. as well as printed works. This Bibliography is being published by the Society in parts.

Dictionaries.—William Marsden printed privately, in 1796, a valuable "Catalogue of Dictionaries, Vocabularies, Grammars, and Alphabets."

Dictionaries.—Trübner's Catalogue of Dictionaries and Grammars (1872, second edition 1882) is a very useful work. H. B. Wheatley's account of English Dictionaries was published in the Transactions of the Philological Society for 1865.

Drama.—A notice of some books in the English Drama will be found in Chapter IV. The *Bibliothèque Dramatique de Mons. de Soleinne* (1843-44, 5 vols.), with its continuation to 1861, is a splendid Catalogue, in which the books are fully described, with valuable notes and preface.

Earthquakes.—Mr. Robert Mallet's Bibliography of Earthquakes will be found in the British Association Report for 1858, and Mons. Alexis Perrey's Bibliographie Seismique in the Dijon *Memoires* for 1855, 1856, and 1861.

Electricity.—Sir Francis Ronalds' Catalogue of Books and Papers relating to Electricity, Magnetism, and the Electric Telegraph (1880) contains a large number of titles. O. Salle's Bibliography of Electricity and Magnetism, 1860 to 1883, was published in 1884.

Entomology.—Dr. Hagen's Bibliotheca Entomologica (Leipzig, 1862-63) is a carefully compiled and useful book.

Epigrams.—There is a list of books connected with Epigrammatic Literature appended to *The Epigrammatists*, by the Rev. Philip Dodd. 8vo. London, 1870.

Fine Art.—The First Proofs of the Universal Catalogue of Books in Art, compiled for the use of the National Art Library and the Schools of Art in the United Kingdom. London, 1870. 2 vols. Sm. 4to. Supplement. London, 1877.

——— Essai d'une Bibliographie de l'Histoire spéciale de la Peinture et de la Gravure en Hollande et en Belgique (1500-1875), par J. F. van Someren, Amsterdam, 1882. 8vo.

Freemasonry.—GOWANS (W.). Catalogue of Books on Freemasonry and kindred subjects. New York, 1858. 8vo.

——— HEMSWORTH (H. W.). Catalogue of Books in the Library at Freemasons' Hall, London. Privately printed.

There is a list of books on Freemasonry in Petzholdt's Bibliotheca Bibliographica, pp. 468–474. Mr. Folkard printed privately a Catalogue of Works on Freemasonry in the Wigan Free Library in 1882, and in the Annals of the Grand Lodge of Iowa, Vol. IX. Part I. (1883) is a Catalogue of Works on this subject in the Library of the Grand Lodge of Iowa.

Future Life.—Catalogue of Works relating to the Nature, Origin, and Destiny of the Soul, by Ezra Abbot. Appended to W. R. Alger's Critical History of the Doctrine of a Future Life. Philadelphia, 1864. 8vo. Reprinted, New York, 1871.

Geography.—See *Voyages and Travels.*

Health.—Catalogue of the International Health Exhibition Library. Division I. Health. Division II. Education. London, 1884. 8vo.

Heraldry.—Thomas Moule's valuable *Bibliotheca Heraldica Magnæ Britanniæ* was published in 1822. There is a "List of the principal English and Foreign Text-Books on Heraldry" at the end of *The Handbook of Heraldry*, by J. E. Cussans, London, 1869.

History (General). — BRUNET (J. C.). Table Methodique en forme de Catalogue raisonné, Histoire. Paris, 1865. 8vo.

—— OETTINGER (E. M.). Historisches Archiv. Archives historiques, contenant une classification de 17,000 ouvrages pour servir à l'étude de l'histoire de tous les siècles et de toutes les nations. Carlsruhe, 1841. 4to.

(Great Britain and Ireland.)—Bishop Nicholson's English, Scotch, and Irish Historical Libraries, 1776, will still be found useful. Mr. Mullinger's portion of the Introduction to the Study of English History (1881) gives the latest information on the subject. Sir Duffus Hardy's "Descriptive Catalogue of Materials relating to the History of Great Britain and Ireland to the end of the reign of Henry VIII." is an invaluable book, but is unfortunately incomplete.

(France.)—LELONG (J.). Bibliothèque Historique (1768-78, 5 vols. folio). "Les Sources de l'Histoire de France," by A. Franklin, was published in 1877.

History (Germany.)—Bibliographical Essay on the Scriptores Rerum Germanicarum, by A. Asher, was published in 1843.

(*Holland.*)—NIJHOFF. Bibliotheca Historico-Neerlandica. La Haye, 1871.

(*Italy.*)—LICHTENTHAL (P.). Manuale Bibliografico del Viaggiatore in Italia. Milano, 1844. A Catalogue of Sir Richard Colt Hoare's Collection of Books relating to the History and Topography of Italy was printed in 1812. The Collection was presented to the British Museum by Hoare in 1825.

(*Portugal.*)—FIGANIERE. Bibliographia Historica Portugueza. Lisboa, 1850.

(*Spain.*)—MUNOZ Y ROMERO. Diccionario bibliografico-historico . . . de Espana. Madrid, 1858.

Language.—See *Dictionaries, Philology.*

Law.—Mr. Stephen R. Griswold contributed an article on Law Libraries to the U.S. Report on Libraries (pp. 161-170). He writes, "Law books may be classified generally as follows : Reports, Treatises, Statute Law. The practice of reporting the decisions of the Judges began in the reign of Edward I., and from that time we have a series of judicial reports of those decisions. In the time of Lord Bacon, these reports extended to fifty or sixty volumes. During the two hundred and fifty years that have passed since then, nothing has been done by way of revision or expurgation ; but these publications have been constantly increasing, so that at the close of the year 1874 the published volumes of reports were as follows: English, 1350 volumes; Irish, 175 volumes; Scotch, 225 volumes; Canadian, 135 volumes; American, 2400 volumes. With respect to treatises (including law periodicals and digests), and without including more than one edition of the same work, it is safe to say that a fair collection would embrace at least 2000 volumes. The statute law of the United States, if confined to the general or revised statutes and codes, may be brought within 100 volumes. If, however, the sessional acts be included, the collection would amount to over 1500 volumes. It is thus seen that a fairly complete law library would embrace more than 7000 volumes, which could not be placed upon its shelves for less than $50,000."

Law.—There is a useful list of legal bibliographies in the "Hand-list of Bibliographies in the Reading-room of the British Museum" (pp. 40-44). Clarke's *Bibliotheca Legum*, which was compiled by Hartwell Horne (1819), is a valuable work. Marvin's *Legal Bibliography*, which was published at Philadelphia in 1847, contains 800 pages. The Catalogue of the Law Library in the New York State Library (1856), forms a useful guide to the subject, and Herbert G. Sweet's "Complete Catalogue of Modern Law Books" is one of the latest catalogues of authority.

Mathematics.—A really good bibliography of Mathematics is still wanting. The following books, however, all from Germany, are useful.

Mathematics.—MURHARD (F. W. A.). Bibliotheca Mathematica. Lipsiæ, 1797-1804. 4 vols.

—— ROGG (J.). Handbuch der Mathematischen Literatur. Tübingen, 1830.

—— SOHNCKE (L. A.). Bibliotheca Mathematica. 1830-54. Leipsic, 1854.

—— ERLECKE (A.). Bibliotheca Mathematica. Halle-a.-S., 1873.

—— Professor De Morgan's Arithmetical Books (1847) is a model of what a good bibliography ought to be.

Medical.—Dr. Billings contributed a chapter on "Medical Libraries in the United States" to the U.S. Report on Public Libraries (pp. 171-182), in which he wrote—" The record of the researches, experiences, and speculations relating to Medical Science during the last four hundred years is contained in between two and three hundred thousand volumes and pamphlets ; and while the immense majority of these have little or nothing of what we call ' practical value,' yet there is no one of them which would not be called for by some inquirer if he knew of its existence." The writer added a list of works of reference which should be in every Medical Library.

There have been a specially large number of Medical Bibliographies, from Haller's works downwards. James Atkinson's Medical Bibliography (1834, A and B only), is an amusing book, but of little or no utility. The most useful books are Dr. Billings's

Index Catalogue of the Library of the Surgeon-General's Office (Washington, 1880) and the Catalogue of the Library of the Royal Medical and Chirurgical Society (3 vols. 1879), by B. R. Wheatley. Neale's Medical Digest (1877) forms a convenient guide to the medical periodicals. The two great French dictionaries — Raige-Delorme and A. Dechambre, Dictionnaire Encyclopédique des Sciences Médicales (4 series, commenced in 1854, and still in progress) ; Jaccoud, Nouveau Dictionnaire de Médecine et de Chirurgie Pratiques (1864, and still in progress) — contain very valuable references to the literature of the various subjects. Of special subjects may be mentioned H. Haeser's Bibliotheca Epidemiographica (1843), John S. Billings's Bibliography of Cholera in the Report of the Cholera Epidemic of 1873 in the United States (1875, pp. 707-1025), Beer's Bibliotheca Ophthalmica (1799), Dr. E. J. Waring's Bibliotheca Therapeutica (1878-79, 2 vols. 8vo.), and Bibliography of Embryology, in Balfour's Embryology, vol. ii.

Meteorology.—A full bibliography of books and papers upon Meteorology is being prepared at the United States Signal Office, and it is reported that 48,000 titles are now in the office. There have been several articles on this subject in, *Symons's Meteorological Magazine*, the last being in the number for December, 1885.

Mineralogy.—DANA (J. D.). Bibliography of Mineralogy. 1881. 8vo.

Mining.—Wigan Free Public Library Index Catalogue of Books and Papers relating to Mining, Metallurgy, and Manufactures. By Henry Tennyson Folkard, Librarian. Southport, 1880. Roy. 8vo.

Motion (Perpetual).—Perpetuum Mobile ; or, search for Self-Motive Power during the 17th, 18th, and 19th centuries, illustrated from various authentic sources in papers, essays, letters, paragraphs, and numerous Patent Specifications, with an Introductory Essay. By Henry Dircks, C.E. London, 1861. Sm. 8vo. Second Series. London, 1870. Sm. 8vo.

Music.—ENGEL (C.). The Literature of National Music. London, 1879. 8vo.

——— Catalogue of the Library of the Sacred Harmonic Society. A new edition [by W. H. Husk]. London, 1872. 8vo.

——— RIMBAULT (F.). Bibliotheca Madrigaliana, a Bibliographical Account of the Musical and Poetical Works published in England during the 16th and 17th centuries, under the titles of Madrigals, Ballets, Ayres, Canzonets, etc. London, 1847. 8vo.

There are bibliographies of the subject in F. L. Ritter's History of Music, London, 1876, and F. Clement, Histoire générale de la Musique Religieuse. Paris, 1861.

Natural History.—Dryander's Catalogue of Sir Joseph Banks's Library, now in the British Museum, is the most famous bibliography of this subject, although made so many years ago. It consists of

5 vols. 8vo. (1798–1800). Vol. 1, General Writers ; Vol. 2, Zoology ; Vol. 3, Botany ; Vol. 4, Mineralogy ; Vol. 5, Supplement.

Natural History.—ENGELMANN (W.). Bibliotheca Historico-Naturalis. Leipzig, 1846.

——— ZUCKOLD (E. A.). Bibliotheca Historico-Naturalis, Physico-Chemica et Mathematica. Göttingen, 1852.

——— See *Zoology.*

Philology.—MARSDEN (W.). Bibliotheca Marsdenia, Philologica et Orientalis. London, 1827. 4to.

——— ENGELMANN (W.). Bibliotheca Philologica. Leipzig, 1853.

——— See *Dictionaries.*

Political Economy.—MCCULLOCH (J. R.). The Literature of Political Economy. London, 1845.— This is a very valuable work up to the date of publication, but a good bibliography of the subject is still a desideratum. The late Professor Stanley Jevons proposed to draw up a Handy Book of the Literature for the Index Society, but, to the great loss of bibliography, was prevented by other work from undertaking it. He contributed a list of Selected Books in Political Economy to the *Monthly Notes* of the Library Association (Vol. 3, No. 7).

Poor.—A Catalogue of Publications in the English Language on subjects relative to the Poor will be found in Eden's *State of the Poor*, vol. iii. pp. ccclxvii—ccclxxxvi.

Printing.—BIGMORE (E. C.), and WYMAN (C. W. H.). A Bibliography of Printing, with Notes and Illustrations. London, 1880. 4to.

—— The Literature of Printing. A Catalogue of the Library illustrative of the History and Art of Typography, Chalcography, and Lithography, by R. M. Hoe. London, 1877. 8vo.

The following is a list of some of the bibliographies of the productions of the chief printers :

Aldus.—Annales de l'Imprimerie des Alde ou Histoire des trois Manuce et de leurs éditions. Par Ant. Aug. Renouard. Paris, an XII. Seconde édition. Paris, 1825. 8vo. 3 vols.

Caxton.—The Life and Typography of William Caxton, England's first Printer, with evidence of his typographical connection with Colard Mansion, the Printer at Bruges. Compiled from original sources by William Blades. London, 1861-63. 2 vols. 4to. A condensed edition was published under the following title : The Biography and Typography of William Caxton, England's first Printer. By William Blades. Second edition. London, 1882. 8vo.

Elzevirs.—Willems (A.). Les Elzevier. Histoire et Annales Typographiques. Bruxelles, 1880. 8vo.

—— C. Pieters. Annales de l'Imprimerie des Elsevier. Gand, 1858. 8vo.

Plantin.—La Maison Plantin à Anvers. Par L. Degeorge. Deuxième édition, augmentée d'une liste chronologique des ouvrages imprimés par Plantin à Anvers de 1555 à 1589. Bruxelles, 1878. 8vo.

Stephens.—Annales de l'Imprimerie des Estienne, ou Histoire de la Famille des Estienne et de ses éditions. Par A. A. Renouard. Paris, 1837-38. 8vo. 2 parts.

Privately Printed Books.—The second edition of John Martin's Bibliographical Catalogue of Privately Printed Books was published in 1854, and a newer work on this important subject is much required. Mr. W. P. Courtney has been engaged in the production of such a work for some years, and the labour could not be in better hands.

Proverbs.—The *Bibliographie Parémiologique* of Pierre Alexandre Gratet-Duplessis (1847), is one of the most elaborate and carefully compiled bibliographies ever published. Sir William Stirling Maxwell printed privately a catalogue of his collection of books of proverbs, in which were specially marked those unknown to Duplessis, or those published since the issue of his catalogue.

Science.—An article on the Scientific Libraries in the United States was contributed by Dr. Theodore Gill to the U.S. Report on Public Libraries (pp. 183-217). It contains an account of the various periodical records of work in the various departments of science.

12

Shorthand.—Thomas Anderson's History of Short-hand, London (1882), contains Lists of Writers on Shorthand in different languages.

Theology.—There is an article on Theological Libraries in the United States, in the U.S. Report on Public Libraries (pp. 127-160). The following extract contains some particulars respecting these.— " There are reported twenty-four libraries, which contain from 10,000 to 34,000 volumes ; and these twenty-four libraries belong to ten different denominations. Three Baptist, two Catholic, two Congregational, three Episcopal, one Lutheran, two Methodist, seven Presbyterian, one Reformed (Dutch), one Reformed (German), and two Unitarian. And, if we include those libraries which contain less than 10,000 volumes, the list of different denominations to which they belong is extended to fifteen or sixteen.''
A considerable number of Bibliographies of Theology will be found in the British Museum Hand-list. Darling's Cyclopædia Bibliographica (1854-59), Malcom's Theological Index (Boston, 1868), and Zuchold's Bibliotheca Theologica (Göttingen, 1864), may be specially mentioned.

Topography.—Gough's British Topography (2 vols. 4to. 1780) is an interesting and useful book, and Upcott's Bibliographical Account of the principal works relating to British Topography, 3 vols. 8vo. (1818), forms one of the best specimens of English bibliography extant.

Topography.—Mr. J. P. Anderson's Book of British Topography (1881) is an indispensable book. Mr. Robert Harrison has prepared for the Index Society an Index of Books on Topography, arranged in one alphabet of places, which has not yet been published. Mr. W. H. K. Wright contributed a paper on "Special Collections of Local Books in Provincial Libraries" to the Transactions of the First Annual Meeting of the Library Association, 1878 (pp. 44-50). Another paper on the same subject, by Mr. J. H. Nodal, appears in the Transactions of the Second Annual Meeting of the Library Association, 1879 (pp. 54-60), entitled "Special Collections of Books in Lancashire and Cheshire," and in the Appendix (pp. 139-148) is a full account of these collections in Public Libraries and private hands.

An indication of some of the chief bibliographies of particular counties and places is here added—

Cornwall : Boase & Courtney, 1874-82. 3 vols. A model bibliography.
Devonshire : J. Davidson, 1852.
    ,,   Plymouth (Three Towns' Bibliotheca), R. N. Worth, 1872-73.
Dorsetshire : C. H. Mayo, privately printed, 1885.
Gloucestershire : Bibliotheca Gloucestrensis, J. Washbourn, 1823-25.

Gloucestershire: Collectanea Glocestriensia, J. D. Phelps, 1842.

Hampshire: Bibliotheca Hantoniensis, H. M. Gilbert, 1872?

,,   List of Books, Sir W. H. Cope, 1879.

Herefordshire : J. Allen, jun., 1821.

Kent : J. Russell Smith, 1837.

Lancashire : H. Fishwick, 1875.

Man (Isle of) : W. Harrison, 1876.

Norfolk : S. Woodward and W. C. Ewing, 1842.

Nottinghamshire : S. F. Creswell, 1863.

Sussex : G. S. Butler, 1866.

Yorkshire: Rt. Hon. John Smythe, Pontefract, 1809.

,,   E. Hailstone, 1858.

,,   W. Boyne, 1869.

Trade and Finance.—Catalogue of Books, comprising the Library of William Paterson, Founder of the Bank of England, in vol. iii. of the Collection of his "Writings, edited by Saxe Bannister," (3 vols. 8vo. London, 1859).

———— Enslin und Engelmann. Bibliothek der Handlungswissenschaft 1750–1845. Leipzig, 1856.

Trials.—The Catalogue of the Library of the Philosophical Institution of Edinburgh (1857) contains (pp. 297-319) a very useful list of trials in an alphabet of the persons tried. The table is arranged under name, charge, date of trial, and reference.

Voyages and Travels.—Locke's Catalogue and character of most books of Voyages and Travels is interesting on account of Locke's notes. (Locke's Works, 1812, 10 vols. 8vo., vol. x. pp. 513-564.)

There are catalogues of books of travels in Pinkerton's collection (1814), and Kerr's collection (1822).

—— Boucher de la Richaderie, Bibliothèque Universelle des Voyages, Paris, 1808. 6 vols. 8vo.

—— Engelmann (W.). Bibliotheca Geographica. Leipzig, 1858.

Zoology. — Agassiz's Bibliographia Zoologicæ et Geologicæ, published by the Ray Society, 1848-54, was a useful book in its day, but it is of no value bibliographically, and the titles being mostly taken at second-hand, the work is full of blunders.

—— Carus and Engelmann's Bibliotheca Zoologica, Leipzig 1861, forms a Supplement to the Bibliotheca Historico-Naturalis of Engelmann.

———

A large number of bibliographies of particular authors have been published in this country and abroad, and it may be useful here to make a note of some of these.

Ariosto, Orlando Furioso: Ulisse Guidi, *Bologna*, 1861, 1868. G. J. Ferrazzi, *Bassano*, 1881.
Boccaccio : M. Landau, *Napoli*, 1881.

Burns : J. Mackie, *Kilmar*, 1866.
Calderon : E. Dorer, *Leipzig*, 1881.
Camoens : Adamson's Life of Camoens, vol. 2, 1820·
Cervantes : E. Dorer, *Leipzig*, 1881.
Corneille : E. Picot, *Paris*, 1876.
Dante : Bibliografia Dantesca, *Prato*, 1845-46. C.
    U. J. Chevalier, 1877. G. A. Scartazzini, Dante
    in Germania, 1881. J. Petzholdt, *Dresden*, 1880.
Goethe : S. Hirzel, 1878.
Luther : E. G. Vogel, *Halle*, 1851. J. Edmands,
    Philadelphia, 1883.
Manzoni : A Vosmara, *Milano*, 1875.
Molière : P. Lacroix, *Paris*, 1875.
Montaigne : J. F. Payer, *Paris*, 1837.
Persius : J. Tarlier, *Bruxelles*, 1848.
Petrarch : Marsand, *Milano*, 1826.
    ,,   A. Hortis, *Trieste*, 1874.
    ,,   G. J. Ferrazzi, *Bassano*, 1877. C. U. J.
    Chevalier, *Montpéliard*, 1880.
Rabelais : J. C. Brunet, *Paris*, 1852.
Schiller : L. Unflad, *München*, 1878.
Tasso : G. J. Ferrazzi, *Bassano*, 1880.
Voltaire : G. Bengesco, *Paris*, 1882.

Browning : F. J. Furnivall, Browning Society, 1881-2.
Carlyle : R. H. Shepherd, 1882.
Defoe : M. Stace, 1829 ; Wilson, 1830 ; Lee, 1862.
Dickens : R. H. Shepherd, 1881.
    ,,   J. Cook, Paisley, 1879.

Hazlitt, Leigh Hunt, Charles Lamb: A. Ireland, 1868.
Ruskin: R. H. Shepherd, 1882.
Shakespeare: J. Wilson, 1827 ; J. O. Halliwell, 1841 ;
    Moulin, 1845 ; Sillig and Ulrici, 1854 ; H. G.
    Bohn, 1864 ; F. Thimm, 1865-72 ; K. Knortz,
    1876 ; Unflad, 1880 ; Justin Winsor (Poems).
Tennyson: R. H. Shepherd, 1879.
Thackeray: R. H. Shepherd, 1881.
Wycliffe: J. Edmands, 1884.

Dr. Garnett commenced a MS. list of such special bibliographies as he came across in Treatises on the different subjects. This list is added to and kept in the Reading Room for use by the Librarians. I was allowed the privilege of referring to this very useful list.

CHAPTER VII.

PUBLISHING SOCIETIES.

 LARGE amount of important information is to be found in the publications of the numerous Societies formed for the purpose of supplying to their subscribers valuable works which are but little likely to find publishers. These publications have in a large number of instances added to our knowledge of history and literature considerably. The Societies have much increased of late years, but no record of the publications is easily to be obtained, since the full account given in Bohn's Supplement to Lowndes's *Bibliographer's Manual*.

The earliest of Publishing Societies was the *Dilettanti Society*, instituted in London in 1734, which issued some fine illustrated volumes of classical travel. A long period of time elapsed without any societies of a similar character being formed.

The Roxburghe Club was formed in the year 1812 in commemoration of the sale of the magnificent library of John third Duke of Roxburghe (died March 19, 1804). It was chiefly intended as a Social Club, and a long list of bibliographical toasts was run through at the banquets. The publications were not at first of any great literary value, although some of them were curious and interesting. After a time competent editors were employed, and some important works produced. Sir Frederick Madden's editions of " Havelok the Dane " was issued in 1828, of the Romance of " William and the Werwolf " in 1832, and of the old English version of " Gesta Romanorum " in 1838. The valuable " Manners and Household Expenses of England in the Thirteeenth and Fifteenth Centuries," edited by T. Hudson Turner, was presented to the Club by Beriah Botfield in 1841 ; Payne Collier's edition of the " Household Books of John Duke of Norfolk, and Thomas Earl of Surrey, 1481–1490," was issued in 1844, and his " Five Old Plays illustrative of the Early Progress of the English Drama " in 1851 ;

the Rev. Joseph Stevenson's edition of "The Owl
and the Nightingale, a Poem of the Twelfth
Century," was issued in 1838, and his edition of
"The Ayenbite of Inwyt" in 1855 ; John Gough
Nichols's edition of the "Literary Remains of King
Edward the Sixth" appeared in 1857 and 1858
(2 vols.), and Dr. Furnivall's edition of Henry
Lonelich's "Seynt Graal" in 1863-1864.

Several years elapsed before the second great
Printing Club was founded. In 1823 *The Bannatyne
Club* was started in Edinburgh, chiefly by Sir Walter
Scott, for the purpose of printing works illustrative
of the History, Antiquities and Literature of Scotland.
It derives its names from George Bannatyne (born
Feb. 22, 1545, died 1607). A long series of books
have been issued by the Club to its members, many
of which are of great interest. The Catalogue of the
Abbotsford Library was presented in 1839 to the
members "by Major Sir Walter Scott, Bart., as
a slight return for their liberality and kindness
in agreeing to continue to that Library the various
valuable works printed under their superintendence."
In the same year appeared Sir Frederick Madden's
edition of *Sir Gawayne*. Bishop Gawin Douglas's
" Palace of Honour" was printed in 1827, and his

translation of Virgil's " Æneid" in 1839 (2 vols.).
The Club was closed in 1867.

The Maitland Club, which derived its name from
Sir Richard Maitland of Lethington (born in 1496,
died March 20, 1586), was instituted in Glasgow in
1828. A volume containing "The Burgh Records of
the City of Glasgow, 1573 to 1581," was presented
to the Club in 1832-34 ; the Poems of Drummond of
Hawthornden in 1832 ; Robert Wodrow's "Collection
upon the Lives of the Reformers and most eminent
Ministers of the Church of Scotland" in 1834-45
(2 vols.). Dauncey's Ancient Scottish Melodies in
1838. Sir Bevis of Hamtoun in the same year, the
Metrical Romance of Lancelot du Lak in 1839 ;
Wodrow's Analecta, or Materials for a History of
Remarkable Providences, in 1842-3 (4 vols.). Henry
Laing's Descriptive Catalogue of Ancient Seals, in
1850. The Club was closed in 1859.

The Abbotsford Club was founded in honour of Sir
Walter Scott in 1834, by Mr. W. B. D. D. Turnbull.
The first book (issued in 1835) was a volume of
"Ancient Mysteries from the Digby MS."; "Arthur
and Merlin, a Metrical Romance," was printed in
1838; "Romances of Sir Guy of Warwick and
Rembrun his Son," in 1840 ; "The Legend of St.

Katherine of Alexandra," in 1841 ; " Sir Degaree, a Metrical Romance of the end of the nineteenth century," in 1849.   The Club was closed in 1866.

These Printing Clubs were select in their constitution, and the books being printed for the members in small numbers, they are difficult to obtain and their price is high.

With the foundation of the Camden Society an entirely new system was adopted, and the general body of book lovers, poor as well as rich, were appealed to with great success, and valuable books were supplied to the subscribers at a price which would have been impossible without such means. The Camden Society is entitled to this honour on account of the general interest of its publications, but the Surtees Society was actually the first to inaugurate the new system.   The subscription fixed was double that which the founders of the Camden Society adopted, but it was, perhaps, a bolder step to start a Society, appealing to a somewhat restricted public with a two guinea subscription, than to appeal to the whole reading public with a subscription of one pound. Before saying more of the Surtees and Camden Societies, it will be necessary to mention some other printing clubs which preceded them.

The Oriental Translation Fund was established in 1828, with the object of publishing Translations from Eastern MSS. into the languages of Europe. When the issue of books was discontinued, the stock of such books as remained was sold off, and many of these can still be obtained at a cheap rate.

The Iona Club was instituted in 1833, for the purpose of investigating the History, Antiquities, and early Literature of the Highlands and Islands of Scotland, but little has been done in the way of publication. The first book was "Collectanea de Rebus Albanicis," and the second, "Transactions of the Club," vol. i. in 4 parts. A second volume was announced, but never appeared.

The Surtees Society was founded at Durham in 1834 for the publication of inedited Manuscripts, illustrative of the moral, the intellectual, the religious, and the social condition of those parts of England and Scotland included on the East, between the Humber and the Frith of Forth, and on the west, between the Mersey and the Clyde, a region which constituted the ancient kingdom of Northumberland. The Society is named after Robert Surtees, of Mainforth, author of the "History of the County Palatine of Durham." Although founded more than fifty years ago, the

Society is still flourishing, and carried on with the
same vigour as of old. The series of publications
is a long one, and contains a large number of most
important works. The second book issued was "Wills
and Inventories, illustrative of the History, Manners,
Language, Statistics, etc., of the Northern Counties
of England, from the Eleventh Century downwards"
(Part 2 was issued in 1860) ; the third, "The Towneley
Mysteries or Miracle Plays"; the fourth, "Testa-
menta Eboracensia : Wills illustrative of the History,
Manners, Language, Statistics, etc., of the Province
of York, from 1300" (vol. 1). The second volume
of this series was issued in 1855. "Anglo-Saxon
and Early English Psalter" was issued in 1843-44
(2 vols.) ; "The Durham Household Book ; or, the
Accounts of the Bursar of the Monastery of Durham,
from 1530 to 1534," in 1844.

The Camden Society, instituted in 1838, has issued to
its subscribers a large number of books of the greatest
interest on historical and literary subjects. The set
of publications is so well known that it is not
necessary to enumerate titles here. Among the most
valuable are the several volumes devoted to the
correspondence of certain old families, such as the
"Plumpton Correspondence" (1839), "Egerton

Papers" (1840), " Rutland Papers " (1842), and
" Savile Correspondence" (1858). The Romances
and Chronicles must also be mentioned, and the
remarkable edition of the oldest English Dictionary,
" Promptorium Parvulorum," which was fully and
learnedly edited by the late Mr. Albert Way. A
second series was commenced in 1871, which is still
continued.

The same year which saw the foundation of the
Camden Society also gave birth to *The English
Historical Society*. Sixteen works of considerable
value were issued, but the greatest of these is the
grand " Codex Diplomaticus Ævi Saxonici" of the
late J. Mitchell Kemble (1845-48).

The Spalding Club, named after John Spalding,
Commissary Clerk of Aberdeen, and founded at
Aberdeen in 1839 for the printing of the Historical,
Ecclesiastical, Genealogical, Topographical, and
Literary Remains of the North-Eastern Counties of
Scotland, was formed on the model of the exclusive
clubs ; but being affected by the more democratic
constitution of the later printing societies, its sub-
scription was fixed at one guinea. Amongst the
most interesting of the Club's publications are the
" Sculptured Stones of Scotland " (1856), " Barbour's

Brus" (1856), and the "Fasti Aberdonensis : Selections from the Records of the University and King's
College of Aberdeen from 1494 to 1854" (1854).

The year 1840 saw the foundation of three very
important Societies, viz. the Parker, the Percy, and
the Shakespeare.

The Parker Society took its name from the famous
Archbishop of Canterbury, Martin Parker, and its
objects were (1) the reprinting, without abridgment,
alteration or omission, of the best works of the
Fathers and early Writers of the Reformed English
Church published in the period between the accession
of Edward VI. and Queen Elizabeth ; (2) the printing
of such works of other writers of the Sixteenth
Century as may appear desirable (including under
both classes some of the early English Translations
of the Foreign Reformers), and (3) the printing of
some MSS. of the same authors hitherto unpublished.
The Society was an enormous success, and at one
time the list contained seven thousand members ; but
owing to the multitude of copies printed, and the
somewhat dry character of the books themselves,
many of them can now be obtained at a ridiculously
small sum, the price of a complete set usually
averaging little more than a shilling a volume. When

the series was completed, a valuable General Index to the whole was compiled by Mr. Henry Gough, 1855.

The Percy Society took its name from Bishop Percy, author of the "Reliques of Ancient English Poetry" (born 1729, died 1811), and was founded for the purpose of bringing to light important but obscure specimens of Ballad Poetry, or Works illustrative of that department of Literature. The Society was dissolved in 1853, but during the thirteen years of its existence it produced a singularly interesting series of publications. The number of separate works registered in Bohn's Appendix to Lowndes's Bibliographer's Manual is 94, besides "Quippes for Upstart New-fangled Gentlewomen by Stephen Gosson," which was suppressed, and "Rhyming Satire on the Pride and Vices of Women Now-a-days, by Charles Bansley," 1540, which was reprinted in 1841, but not issued. The set is much sought after, and fetches a good price.

The Shakespeare Society was founded in 1840, to print books illustrative of Shakespeare and of the literature of his time, and a very valuable collection of works was issued to the subscribers during the term of its existence. It was dissolved in 1853, and the remaining stock was made up into volumes and

13

sold off. There was much for the Society still to do ;
but the controversy arising out of the discovery of the
forgeries connected with John Payne Collier's name
made it difficult for the Shakespearians to work
together with harmony.

In this same year the *Musical Antiquarian Society*
was founded, and during the seven years of its existence it issued books of Madrigals, Operas, Songs,
Anthems, etc., by early English composers.

In the following year (1841), the *Motett Society* was
founded for the publication of Ancient Church Music.
Five parts only, edited by Dr. Rimbault, were issued.

In 1841 the *Society for the Publication of Oriental
Texts* was founded, and a series of works in Syriac,
Arabic, Sanscrit, and Persian was distributed to the
subscribers until 1851, when the Society was dissolved.

The Wodrow Society was instituted in Edinburgh
in 1841, for the publication of the early writers of the
Reformed Church of Scotland, and named after the
Rev. Robert Wodrow.   Among its publications
are, " Autobiography and Diary of James Melvill,"
" Correspondence of the Rev. R. Wodrow " (3 vols.),
" History of the Reformation in Scotland, by John
Knox " (2 vols.).   The Society was dissolved in
1848.

The Ælfric Society was founded in 1842 for the publication of those Anglo-Saxon and other literary monuments, both civil and ecclesiastical, tending to illustrate the early state of England. The publications, which were not numerous, were edited by Benjamin Thorpe and J. M. Kemble, and the Society was discontinued in 1856.

The Chetham Society, founded at Manchester in 1843, for the publication of Historical and Literary remains connected with the Palatine Counties of Lancaster and Chester, was named after Humphrey Chetham (born 1580, died 1653). The Society, which still flourishes, has now produced a very long series of important works, and the volumes, which are not often met with, keep up their price well.

The Sydenham Society for reprinting Standard English Works in Medical Literature, and for the Translation of Foreign Authors, with notes, was founded in 1843. After printing a number of important works, the Society was dissolved in 1858, and was succeeded by *The New Sydenham Society*.

The Spottiswoode Society was founded at Edinburgh in 1843, for the revival and publication of the acknowledged works of the Bishops, Clergy, and Laity of the Episcopal Church of Scotland, and rare, authentic, and curious MSS., Pamphlets and other Works illustrative of the Civil and Ecclesiastical State of Scotland. It takes its name from John Spottiswoode, the first duly consecrated Scottish Archbishop after the Reformation (born 1566, died 1639.) The late Mr. Hill Burton gives an amusing account of the foundation of this Society in his delightful *Book-Hunter.* He writes : " When it was proposed to establish an institution for reprinting the works of the fathers of the Episcopal Church in Scotland, it was naturally deemed that no more worthy or characteristic name could be attached to it than that of the venerable prelate, who by his learning and virtues had so long adorned the Episcopal Chair of Moray and Ross [Robert Jolly], and who had shown a special interest in the department of literature to which the institution was to be devoted. Hence it came to pass that, through a perfectly natural process, the Association for the purpose of reprinting the works of certain old divines was to be ushered into the world by the style and title of the JOLLY CLUB. There happened to be amongst those concerned, however, certain persons so corrupted with the wisdom of this world, as to apprehend that the miscellaneous public might fail to trace this designa-

tion to its true origin, and might indeed totally
mistake the nature and object of the institution,
attributing to it aims neither consistent with the
ascetic life of the departed prelate, nor with the pious
and intellectual object of its founders. The counsels
of these worldly-minded persons prevailed. The
Jolly Club was never instituted,—at least as an
association for the reprinting of old books of divinity,—
though I am not prepared to say that institutions,
more than one so designed may not exist for other
purposes. The object, however, was not entirely
abandoned. A body of gentlemen united themselves
together under the name of another Scottish prelate,
whose fate had been more distinguished, if not more
fortunate, and the Spottiswoode Society was established. Here, it will be observed, there was a
passing to the opposite extreme, and so intense seems
to have been the anxiety to escape from all excuse
for indecorous jokes or taint of joviality, that the
word Club, wisely adopted by other bodies of the
same kind, was abandoned, and this one called itself
a Society." The publications were discontinued
about 1851.

The Calvin Translation Society was established at
Edinburgh in 1843, and its work was completed in

1855, by the publication of twenty-two Commentaries, etc., of the great reformer in fifty-two volumes.

The Ray Society was founded in 1844 for the publication of works on Natural History (Zoology and Botany), and a large number of valuable books, fully illustrated, have been produced, many of them translations from foreign works. Many of the later publications are more elaborately coloured than the earlier ones.

The Wernerian Club was instituted in 1844 for the republication of standard works of Scientific Authors of old date.

The Handel Society was founded at London in 1844, for the purpose of printing the Works of Handel in full score. Sixteen volumes were issued, and in 1858 the Society was dissolved, the German Handel Society resuming the publication.

The Hanserd Knollys Society was instituted in 1845 for the publication of the works of early English and other Baptist writers, and one of these was an edition of Bunyan's Pilgrim Progress from the text of the first edition. The Society was dissolved about 1851.

The Caxton Society was instituted in 1845 for

the publication of Chronicles and other writings hitherto unpublished, illustrative of the history and miscellaneous literature of the middle ages. This Society was formed on a somewhat original basis. The members were to pay no annual subscription, but they engaged to purchase one copy of all books published by the Society. The expense of printing and publishing to be defrayed out of the proceeds of the sale, and the money remaining over to be paid to the editors.

The Cavendish Society was instituted in 1846 for the promotion of Chemical Science by the translation and publication of valuable works and papers on Chemistry not likely to be undertaken by ordinary publishers. During its last years the Society existed for the publication of Gmelin's voluminous "Handbook of Chemistry," and when this work was completed, with a general Index, the Society ceased to exist.

The Ecclesiastical History Society was instituted in 1846, and one of its early publications was the first volume of Wood's "Athenæ Oxoniensis," edited by Dr. Bliss, but this only contained the life of Anthony Wood himself. The Society was dissolved in 1854, after publishing the Book of Common Prayer according to a MS. in the Rolls Office, Dublin (3 vols.), and sundry other works.

The Hakluyt Society, named after Richard Hakluyt (born 1553, died 1616), was founded at the end of 1846 for the purpose of printing the most rare and valuable Voyages, Travels and Geographical Records, from an early period of exploratory enterprise to the circumnavigation of Dampier. The first two volumes ("Sir Richard Hawkins's Voyage into the South Sea, 1593," and "Select Letters of Columbus") were issued in 1847, and the Society still flourishes. Between 1847 and 1885 the Society has presented to its members an important series of books of travel, at the rate of about two volumes a year for an annual subscription of one guinea.

The Palæontographical Society was founded in 1847 for the purpose of figuring and describing a stratigraphical series of British Fossils. The annual volumes consist of portions of works by the most eminent palæontologists, and these works are completed as soon as circumstances allow, but several of them are still incomplete.

The Arundel Society is so important an institution that it cannot be passed over in silence, although, as

the publications chiefly consist of engravings, chromo-
lithographs, etc., it scarcely comes within the scope of
this chapter. The Society takes its name from Thomas
Howard Earl of Arundel, in the reigns of James I.
and Charles I., who has been styled the "Father of
vertu in England." It was founded in 1849, and its
purpose is to diffuse more widely, by means of suitable
publications, a knowledge both of the history and
true principles of Painting, Sculpture, and the higher
forms of ornamental design, to call attention to such
masterpieces of the arts as are unduly neglected, and
to secure some transcript or memorial of those which
are perishing from ill-treatment or decay. The publications of the Society have been very successful, and
many of them cannot now be obtained.

Most of the societies above described have appealed
to a large public, and endeavoured to obtain a large
amount of public support; but in 1853 was formed an
exclusive society, with somewhat the same objects as
the Roxburghe Club. *The Philobiblon Society* was
instituted chiefly through the endeavours of Mr. R.
Monckton Milnes (the late Lord Houghton) and the
late Mons. Sylvain Van de Weyer. The number of
members was at first fixed at thirty-five, but was raised
in 1857 to forty, including the patron and honorary

secretaries. The publications consist chiefly of a series of Bibliographical and Historical Miscellanies, contributed by the members, which fill several volumes. Besides these there are " The Expedition to the Isle of Rhe by Lord Herbert of Cherbury," edited and presented to the members by the Earl of Powis ; "Inventaire de tous les meubles du Cardinal Mazarin," edited and presented by H.R.H. the Duke d'Aumale ; " Memoires de la Cour d'Espagne sous la regne de Charles II., 1678–82," edited and presented by William Stirling (afterwards Sir William Stirling Maxwell) ; " The Biography and Bibliography of Shakespeare," compiled and presented by Henry G. Bohn ; " Analyse des Travaux de la Société des Philobiblon de Londres," par Octave Delepierre.

The Ossianic Society was instituted at Dublin in 1853 for the preservation and publication of manu-scripts in the Irish Language, illustrative of the Fenian period of Irish history, etc., with literal translations and notes.

The Warton Club was instituted in 1854 and issued four volumes, after which it was dissolved.

The Manx Society was instituted at Douglas, Isle of Man, in 1858, for the publication of National Documents of the Isle of Man.

All the Societies mentioned above are registered in Henry Bohn's Appendix to Lowndes's Bibliographer's Manual, and lists of the publications up to 1864 are there given. Most of them are also described in Hume's " Learned Societies and Printing Clubs of the United Kingdom" (1853). Since, however, the publication of these two books, a considerable number of important Printing Societies have been formed, and of these a list is not readily obtainable, except by direct application to the respective Secretaries.

The newly printed General Catalogue of the British Museum in the Reading Room however contains a full list of the publications of the various Societies under the heading of *Academies*.

The foundation of the *Early English Text Society* in 1864 caused a renewed interest to be taken in the publications of the Printing Clubs. The origin of the Society was in this wise. When the Philological Society undertook the formation of a great English Dictionary, the want of printed copies of some of the

chief monuments of the language was keenly felt.
Mr. F. J. Furnivall, with his usual energy, determined
to supply the want, and induced the Council of the
Philological Society to produce some valuable texts.
It was found, however, that these publications exhausted
much of the funds of the Society, which was required
for the printing of the papers read at the ordinary
meetings, so that it became necessary to discontinue
them.   Mr. Furnivall, then, in conjunction with
certain members of the Philological Society, founded
the Early English Text Society.   The Society
possessed the inestimable advantage of having among
its founders Mr. Richard Morris (afterwards the Rev.
Dr. Morris), who entered with fervour into the
scheme, and produced a large amount of magnificent
work for the Society.   Dr. Furnivall put the objects
of the Society forward very tersely when he said that
none of us should rest " till Englishmen shall be able
to say of their early literature what the Germans can
now say with pride of theirs—'every word of it is
printed, and every word of it is glossed.'"

The Society prospered, and in 1867 an Extra Series
was started, in which were included books that had
already been printed, but were difficult to obtain from
their rarity and price.

One hundred and twenty-six volumes have been issued between 1864 and 1884, eighty-two volumes of the Original Series and forty-four of the Extra Series, and there can be no doubt that the publications of the Society have had an immense influence in fostering the study of the English language. The prefaces and glossaries given with each work contain an amount of valuable information not elsewhere to be obtained.

These books throw light upon the growth of the language, and place within the reach of a large number of readers works of great interest in the literature of the country. The greatest work undertaken by the Society is the remarkable edition of " William's Vision of Piers the Plowman," which Prof. Skeat has produced with an expenditure of great labour during nearly twenty years. The last part, containing elaborate notes and glossary, was issued in 1884.

The subjects treated of are very various. There is a fair sprinkling of Romances, which will always be amongst the most interesting of a Society's publications. Manners and Customs are largely illustrated in a fair proportion of the Texts, as also are questions of Social and Political History. Perhaps the least interesting to the general reader are the Theological Texts, which are numerous, but the writers of these were thoroughly imbued with the spirit of their times, and although they are apt to be prosy, they are pretty sure to introduce some quaint bits which compensate for a considerable amount of dulness. These books help us to form a correct idea of the beliefs of our forefathers, and to disabuse our minds of many mistaken views which we have learnt from more popular but less accurate sources.

The Ballad Society grew out of the publication, by special subscription, of Bishop Percy's Folio Manuscript, edited by F. J. Furnivall and J. W. Hales. This was issued in connection with the Early English Text Society (but not as one of its Texts), through the energy of Mr. Furnivall, who had many difficulties to overcome before he was able to get permission to print the manuscript, which had been very faithfully guarded from the eyes of critics. He had to pay for the privilege, and in the end the old volume was sold to the nation, and it now reposes among the treasures of the British Museum. When this useful work was completed, Mr. Furnivall was anxious to follow it by a reprint of all the known collections of Ballads, such as the Roxburghe, Bagford, Rawlinson, Douce, etc., and for this purpose he started the Ballad Society in 1868. He himself edited some particularly interesting

" Ballads from Manuscripts," and an elaborate account
of Captain Cox's Ballads and Books in a new edition
of Robert Laneham's Letter on the Entertainment at
Kenilworth in 1575. The veteran Ballad illustrator,
Mr. William Chappell, undertook to edit the " Rox-
burghe Ballads," and produced nine parts, when the
Rev. J. W. Ebsworth took the work off his hands.
Mr. Ebsworth had previously reproduced the "Bagford
Ballads," and he is now the editor-in-chief of the
Society. The following is a short list of the publica-
tions of the Society : Nos. 1, 2, 3, 10, " Ballads from
Manuscripts " ; Nos. 4, 5, 6, 8, 9, 12, 13, 18, 19.
" The Roxburghe Ballads," edited by Wm. Chappell;
No. 7, " Captain Cox, his Ballads and Books " ; No.
11, " Love Poems and Humourous Ones " ; Nos.
14, 15, 16, 17, " The Bagford Ballads." No. 20,
" The Amanda Group of Bagford Ballads ; " Nos.
21, 22, 23, 24, 25, 26, " The Roxburghe Ballads,"
edited by the Rev. J. W. Ebsworth. No. 26 com-
pletes the fifth volume of the " Roxburghe Ballads."
There are two more volumes to come, and then Mr.
Ebsworth will undertake " The Civil War and
Protectorate Ballads." Much of the work on these
volumes is done, and they only await an increase in
the subscription list. It is to be hoped that when the

good work done by the Ballad Society is better known, the editor will not be kept back in his useful course by the want of funds for printing.   Mr. Ebsworth's thorough work is too well known to need praise here, but it may be noted that his volumes contain a remarkable amount of illustration of the manners of the time not to be obtained elsewhere.   The value of this is the more apparent by the system of arrangement in marked periods which the editor has adopted.

The Chaucer Society was founded in 1868 by Mr. Furnivall, "to do honour to Chaucer, and to let the lovers and students of him see how far the best un-printed Manuscripts of his Works differed from the printed texts."   For the Canterbury Tales, Mr. Furnivall has printed the six best unprinted MSS. in two forms—(1) in large oblong parts, giving the parallel texts ; (2) in octavo, each text separately. The six manuscripts chosen are—The Ellesmere ; The Lansdowne (Brit. Mus.) ; The Hengwrt ; The Corpus, Oxford ; The Cambridge (University Library); The Petworth.   Dr. Furnivall has now added Harleian 7334 to complete the series.   The Society's publications are issued in two series, of which the first contains the different Texts of Chaucer's Works,

and the second such originals of and essays on these
as can be procured, with other illustrative treatises
and Supplementary Tales.

The Spenser Society was founded at Manchester in
1867 for the publication of well-printed editions of
old English authors in limited numbers. The chief
publication issued to subscribers was a reprint, in
three volumes folio, of the works of John Taylor,
the Water-poet, from the original folio. The other
publications are in small quarto, and among them are
the works of John Taylor not included in the folio,
the works of Wither, etc.

The Roxburghe Library was a subscription series,
commenced by Mr. W. Carew Hazlitt in 1868, with
the same objects as a publishing society. It was
discontinued in 1870. The following is a list of the
publications :—" Romance of Paris and Vienne ";
William Browne's Complete Works," 2 vols.; "Inedited Tracts of the 16th and 17th Centuries (1579-
1618) "; "The English Drama and Stage under the
Tudor and Stuart Princes, 1543-1664 "; "George
Gascoigne's Complete Poems," 2 vols.; "Thomas
Carew's Poems."

The Harleian Society was founded in 1869. Their
chief publication has been the late Colonel Chester's

14

magnificently edited Registers of Westminster Abbey.
Other Registers published are those of St. Peter's,
Cornhill ; St. Dionis Backchurch ; St. Mary Alder-
mary ; St. Thomas the Apostle ; St. Michael, Corn-
hill ; St. Antholin, Budge Lane ; and St. John the
Baptist, on Wallbrook.   Of the other publications
there are Visitations of Bedfordshire, Cheshire, Corn-
wall, Cumberland, Devon, Essex, Leicestershire,
London 1568, 1633, Nottingham, Oxford, Rutland,
Somersetshire, Warwickshire, and Yorkshire, and
Le Neve's Catalogue of Knights.

The Hunterian Club was founded at Glasgow in
1871, and named after the Hunterian Library in the
University.   Among the publications of the Club are
a Series of Tracts by Thomas Lodge and Samuel
Rowlands ; the Poetical Works of Alexander Craig ;
Poetical Works of Patrick Hannay ; Sir T. Over-
burie's Vision by Richard Niccols, 1616. The printing
of the famous Bannatyne Manuscript, compiled by
George Bannatyne, 1568, was commenced by the
Society in 1873, and the seventh part, which completed this invaluable collection of Scottish Poetry,
was issued in 1881.

The Folk Lore Society was founded by the late Mr.
W. J. Thoms (inventor of the term Folk Lore) in

1878, and during the seven years of its existence it has done much valuable work, chiefly through the energetic direction of Mr. G. L. Gomme, the Hon. Sec. (now Director). The object of the Society is stated to be "the preservation and publication of Popular Traditions, Legendary Ballads, Local Proverbial Sayings, Superstitions and Old Customs (British and Foreign), and all subjects relating to them." The principal publication of the Society, the *Folk Lore Record*, now the *Folk Lore Journal*, was at first issued in volumes, and afterwards in monthly numbers. It is now a quarterly. The other publications are :— Henderson's Folk-Lore of the Northern Counties of England and the Borders, a new edition ; Aubrey's Remaines of Gentilisme and Judaisme ; Gregor's Notes on the Folk-Lore of the North-east of Scotland ; Comparetti's Book of Sindibad and Pedroso's Portuguese Folk Tales ; Black's Folk Medicine ; Callaway's Religious System of the Amazulu.

The year 1873 saw the formation of several publishing Societies.

The New Shakspere Society was founded by Dr. F. J. Furnivall, for the reading of papers, which have been published in a Series of Transactions, and also for the publication of collations of the Quarto Plays, and

works illustrating the great Dramatist's times. Among
the latter works are Harrison's Description of England,
Stubbes's Anatomie of Abuses, Dr. Ingleby's Shakespeare's Centurie of Prayse, etc.

The English Dialect Society was founded at Cambridge by the Rev. Professor Skeat.   Its objects are
stated to be (1) to bring together all those who have
made a study of any of the Provincial Dialects of
England, or who are interested in the subject of
Provincial English ; (2) to combine the labours
of collectors of Provincial English words by providing
a common centre to which they may be sent, so as to
gather material for a general record of all such words ;
(3) to publish (subject to proper revision) such collections of Provincial English words that exist at present
only in manuscript ; as well as to reprint such
Glossaries of provincial words as are not generally
accessible, or are inserted in books of which the
main part relates to other subjects ; and (4) to supply
references to sources of information which may be of
material assistance to word-collectors, students, and
all who have a general or particular interest in the
subject.   The publications are arranged under the
following Series : A, Bibliographical ; B, Reprinted
Glossaries ; C, Original Glossaries ; D, Miscellaneous.

In 1875 the Society was transferred to Manchester, and Mr. J. H. Nodal became Honorary Secretary.

The Palæographical Society was formed for the purpose of reproducing Specimens of Manuscripts, and it has produced a Series of Facsimiles of Ancient Manuscripts, edited by E. A. Bond and E. M. Thompson, Part 1 being issued in 1873.

At the end of the year 1877 *The Index Society* was founded for the purpose of producing (1) Indexes of Standard Works; (2) Subject Indexes of Science, Literature and Art; and (3) a General Reference Index. The publications were commenced in 1878, and the First Annual Meeting was held in March, 1879, the Earl of Carnarvon being the first President. The first publication was "What is an Index?" by H. B. Wheatley. Among the important books issued by the Society may be mentioned Solly's "Index of Hereditary Titles of Honour"; Daydon Jackson's "Guide to the Literature of Botany" and "Literature of Vegetable Technology," and Rye's "Index of Norfolk Topography."

The *Society for the Promotion of Hellenic Studies* was founded in 1879 for the following objects : (1) To advance the study of the Greek language, literature, and art, and to illustrate the history of the Greek race in the ancient, Byzantine, and Neo-Hellenic periods, by the publication of memoirs and inedited documents or monuments in a Journal to be issued periodically. (2) To collect drawings, facsimiles, transcripts, plans, and photographs of Greek inscriptions, MSS., works of art, ancient sites and remains, and with this view to invite travellers to communicate to the Society notes or sketches of archæological and topographical interest. (3) To organise means by which members of the Society may have increased facilities for visiting ancient sites and pursuing archæological researches in countries which, at any time, have been the sites of Hellenic civilization. Five volumes of the *Journal* have been issued.

The Topographical Society of London was formed in 1880. The Inaugural Meeting was held at the Mansion House, and the first Annual Meeting at Drapers' Hall on Feb. 3, 1882, with the Lord Mayor (Sir John Whitaker Ellis), President, in the chair. The following reproductions have been issued to subscribers :—Van der Wyngaerde's View of London, ab. 1550, 7 sheets; Braun & Hogenberg's Plan of London, 1 sheet; Visscher's View of London, 4 sheets.

The Browning Society was founded by Dr. Furnivall

in 1881, and besides papers read at the meetings, the Society has issued Dr. Furnivall's " Bibliography of Browning."

The Wyclif Society was founded also by Dr. Furnivall in 1882, for the publication of the complete works of the great Reformer.

The Pipe Roll Society was established in 1883, and in 1885 the first three volumes of its publications have been issued to the members. These are—Vol. 1, Pipe Rolls, 5 Hen. II.; Vol. 2, 6 Hen. II.; Vol. 3, Introduction.

The Oxford Historical Society was formed in 1884, and four handsome volumes have been issued for that year and 1885. These are—1, "Register of the University of Oxford" (vol. 1, 1449-63, 1505-71), edited by the Rev. C. W. Boase ; 2, "Remarks and Collections of Thomas Hearne" (vol. 1, July 4, 1705–March, 19, 1707), edited by C. E. Doble, M.A. Both these volumes are supplied with temporary Indexes. 3, "The Early History of Oxford, 727–1100," by James Parker ; 4, "Memories of Merton College," by the Hon. George C. Brodrick ; 5, "Collectanea." First Series. Edited by C. R. L. Fletcher.

The Middlesex County Record Society was formed in

1885 "for the purpose of publishing the more interesting portions of the old County Records of
Middlesex, which have lately been arranged and
calendared by order of the Justices." Nothing has
been published as yet, but Mr. Cordy Jeaffreson is
engaged upon the first two volumes, one of which
will be issued shortly.

The Rev. Dr. A. B. Grosart has himself printed by
subscription more works of our Old Writers than
many a Society, and therefore it is necessary to
mention his labours here, although a complete list of
them cannot be given. The chief series are : " The
Fuller Worthies Library," 39 volumes ; " The
Chertsey Worthies Library," 14 vols. 4to., and
" The Huth Library."

CHAPTER VIII.

CHILD'S LIBRARY.

HE idea of a Child's Library is to a great extent modern, and it is not altogether clear that it is a good one, except in the case of those children who have no books of their own. It is far better that each child should have his own good books, which he can read over and over again, thus thoroughly mastering their contents.

It is a rather wide-spread notion that there is some sort of virtue in reading for reading's sake, although really a reading boy may be an idle boy. When a book is read, it should be well thought over before another is begun, for reading without thought generates no ideas.

One advantage of a Child's Library should be that the reader is necessarily forced to be careful, so as to return the books uninjured. This is a very important point, for children should be taught from their earliest years to treat books well, and not to destroy them as they often do. We might go farther than this and say that children should be taught at school how to handle a book. It is really astonishing to see how few persons (not necessarily children) among those who have not grown up among books know how to handle them. It is positive torture to a man who loves books to see the way they are ordinarily treated. Of course it is not necessary to mention the crimes of wetting the fingers to turn over the leaves, or turning down pages to mark the place; but those who ought to know better will turn a book over on its face at the place where they have left off reading, or will turn over pages so carelessly that they give a crease to each which will never come out.

For a healthy education it is probably best that a child should have the run of

a library for adults (always provided that
dangerous books are carefully excluded).
A boy is much more likely to enjoy and find
benefit from the books he selects himself
than from those selected for him.

The circumstances of the child should be
considered in the selection of books; thus
it is scarcely fair when children are working
hard at school all day that they should be
made to read so-called instructive books in
the evening. They have earned the right
to relaxation and should be allowed good
novels. To some boys books of Travels and
History are more acceptable than novels,
but all children require some Fiction, and,
save in a few exceptional cases, their
imaginations require to be cultivated.

It will soon be seen whether children
have healthy or unhealthy tastes. If healthy,
they are best left to themselves; if unhealthy,
they must be directed.

It is easy for the seniors to neglect the
children they have under them, and it is
easy to direct them overmuch, but it is
difficult to watch and yet let the children

go their own way. We are apt, in arranging
for others, to be too instructive; nothing is
less acceptable to children or less likely
to do them good than to be preached at.
Moral reflections in books are usually
skipped by children, and unless somewhat
out of the common, probably by grown-up
persons as well. Instruction should grow
naturally out of the theme itself, and form
an integral part of it, so that high aims
and noble thoughts may naturally present
themselves to the readers.

One of the chapters in the United States
Libraries' Report is on "School and Asylum
Libraries" (pp. 38–59), in which we are
informed that New York was the pioneer
in founding school libraries. "In 1827
Governor De Witt Clinton, in his message to
the legislature, recommended their formation; but it was not till 1835 that the friends
of free schools saw their hopes realized in
the passage of a law which permitted the
voters in any school district to levy a tax of
$20 to begin a library, and a tax of $10 each
succeeding year to provide for its increase."

Another chapter in the same Report is on " Public Libraries and the Young" (pp. 412– 418), in which Mr. Wm. J. Fletcher advocates the use of the library as an addition to the school course. He writes, " It only remains now to say that, as we have before intimated, the public library should be viewed as an adjunct of the public school system, and to suggest that in one or two ways the school may work together with the library in directing the reading of the young. There is the matter of themes for the writing of compositions; by selecting subjects on which information can be had at the library, the teacher can send the pupil to the library as a student, and readily put him in communication with, and excite his interest in, classes of books to which he has been a stranger and indifferent."

A very interesting book on this subject is entitled "Libraries and Schools. Papers selected by Samuel S. Green. New York (F. Leypoldt), 1883." It contains the following subjects: "The Public Library and the Public Schools;" "The Relation of the

Public Library to the Public Schools";
"Libraries as Educational Institutions";
"The Public Library as an Auxiliary to the
Public Schools"; "The Relation of Libraries
to the School System"; and "A Plan of
Systematic Training in Reading at School."

"*Books for the Young, a Guide for Parents
and Children.* Compiled by C. M. Hewins.
New York (F. Leypoldt), 1882," is an
extremely useful little book. It contains
a valuable list of books arranged in classes.
Certain marks are used to indicate the
character of the books, thus the letter (*c*)
indicates that the book is especially suitable
for children under ten, (*b*) that it is especially suitable for boys, and (*g*) that it is
especially suitable for girls.

Prefixed are eight sensible rules as to
how to teach the right use of books.

Perkins's "Best Reading" contains a
good list of books for children (pp. 299–
303).

The children's books of the present day
are so beautifully produced that the elders
are naturally induced to exclaim, "We never

had such books as these," but probably we enjoyed our books as well as our children do theirs. What a thrill of pleasure the middle-aged man feels when a book which amused his childhood comes in his way : this, however, is seldom, for time has laid his decaying hand upon them—

" All, all are gone, the old familiar faces."

The children for whom Miss Kate Greenaway and Mr. Caldecott draw and Mrs. Gatty and Mrs. Ewing wrote are indeed fortunate, but we must not forget that Charles and Mary Lamb wrote delightful books for the young, that Miss Edgeworth's stories are ever fresh, and that one of the most charming children's stories ever written is Mrs. Sherwood's *Little Woodman.*

A short list of a Child's Library is quoted in the *Library Journal* (vol. viii. p. 57) from the *Woman's Journal.* The family for whom it was chosen consisted of children from three to twelve, the two eldest being girls. The books are mostly American, and but little known in this country—

Snow-bound. Illustrated. Whittier.
Life of Longfellow.   Kennedy.
A Summer in the Azores.   Baker.
Among the Isles of Shoals. Celia Thaxter.
The boys of '76.   Coffin.
The boys of '61.   Coffin.
Story of our Country.   Higginson.
Sir Walter Raleigh.   Towle.
Child's History of England.   Dickens.
Tales from Shakespear.   Lamb.
Tales from Homer.   Church.
The Wonder-book. Illustrated. Hawthorne.
Young folks' book of poetry.   Campbell.
Poetry for childhood.   Eliot.
Bits of talk about home matters.   H. H.
The Seven Little Sisters.   Andrews.
Hans Brinker, or the Silver Skates. Dodge.
Room for one more.   Mary T. Higginson.
King Arthur for boys.   Lanier.
Doings of the Bodley family.   Scudder.
Mother-play and Nursery-rhymes.
Children's Robinson Crusoe.
The four-footed lovers.
Mammy Tittleback and her family. H. H.
The Little Prudy books.   Six volumes.

The editor of the *Library Journal* remarks on the list, "Guest's Lectures on English History is better than Dickens's, and the 'Prudy' children are so mischievous, so full of young Americanisms, and so far from being 'wells of English undefiled,' that they are not always good companions for boys and girls. I have known a child's English spoiled by reading the Prudy books."

Some of the old-fashioned children's books have been reprinted, and these will generally be found very acceptable to healthy-minded children, but some of the old books are not easily met with. No Child's Library should be without a good collection of Fairy Tales, a careful selection of the Arabian Nights, or Robinson Crusoe. Gulliver's Travels is very unsuited for children, although often treated as a child's book. Berquin's *Children's Friend*, Edgeworth's *Parent's Assistant* and the Aikins's *Evenings at Home*, will surely still amuse children, although some may think their teaching too didactic. It is only by practical experience that we can tell what children will like.

Sandford and Merton is, I believe, usually considered as hopelessly out of date, but I have found young hearers follow my reading of it with the greatest interest. *The Pilgrim's Progress* will always have as great a fascination for the young as it must have for their elders; but there is much preaching in it which must be skipped, or the attention of the hearers will flag.

CHAPTER X.

One Hundred Books.

IN the Fourth Chapter of this Volume two lists of selected books are given, viz. The Comtist's Library, and a list of one hundred good novels. Since that chapter was written and printed, much public attention has been drawn to this branch of our subject by the publication of Sir John Lubbock's list of books which he recommended to the members of the Working Men's College, when he lectured at that place on "Books." The comments by eminent men, which have appeared in the *Pall Mall Gazette*, have also attracted attention, and it seems desirable that some note on this list should appear in these pages.

The list issued by the *Pall Mall Gazette* is as follows:

NON-CHRISTIAN MORALISTS.

Marcus Aurelius, *Meditations.*
Epictetus, *Encheiridion.*
Confucius, *Analects.*
Aristotle, *Ethics.*
Mahomet, *Koran.*

THEOLOGY AND DEVOTION.

Apostolic Fathers, *Wake's Collection.*
St. Augustine, *Confessions.*
Thomas à Kempis, *Imitation.*
Pascal, *Pensées.*
Spinoza, *Tractatus Theologico-Politicus.*
Butler, *Analogy.*
Jeremy Taylor, *Holy Living and Holy Dying.*
Keble, *Christian Year.*
Bunyan, *Pilgrim's Progress.*

CLASSICS.

Aristotle, *Politics.*
Plato, *Phædo* and *Republic.*
Æsop, *Fables.*
Demosthenes, *De Coronâ.*
Lucretius.
Plutarch.
Horace.
Cicero, *De Officiis, De Amicitiâ,* and *De Senectute.*

Epic Poetry.
Homer, *Iliad* and *Odyssey.*
Hesiod.
Virgil.
Niebelungenlied.
Malory, *Morte d'Arthur.*

Eastern Poetry.
Mahabharata and *Ramayana* (epitomised by Talboys Wheeler).
Firdausi, *Shah-nameh* (translated by Atkinson).
She-king (Chinese Odes).

Greek Dramatists.
Æschylus, *Prometheus, The House of Atreus, Trilogy,* or *Persæ.*
Sophocles, *Œdipus,* Trilogy.
Euripides, *Medea.*
Aristophanes, *The Knights.*

History.
Herodotus.
Thucydides.
Xenophon, *Anabasis.*
Tacitus, *Germania.*
Gibbon, *Decline and Fall.*
Voltaire, *Charles XII.* or *Louis XIV.*
Hume, *England.*
Grote, *Greece.*

Philosophy.
Bacon, *Novum Organum.*

Mill, *Logic* and *Political Economy.*
Darwin, *Origin of Species.*
Smith, *Wealth of Nations* (selection).
Berkeley, *Human Knowledge.*
Descartes, *Discourse sur la Méthode.*
Locke, *Conduct of the Understanding.*
Lewes, *History of Philosophy.*

TRAVELS.

Cook, *Voyages.*
Darwin, *Naturalist in the Beagle.*

POETRY AND GENERAL LITERATURE.

Shakspeare.
Milton.
Dante.
Spenser.
Scott.
Wordsworth.
Pope.
Southey.
Longfellow.
Goldsmith, *Vicar of Wakefield.*
Swift, *Gulliver's Travels.*
Defoe, *Robinson Crusoe.*
The Arabian Nights.
Don Quixote.
Boswell, *Johnson.*
Burke, *Select Works.*
Essayists—Addison, Hume, Montaigne, Macaulay,
    Emerson.

Molière.
Sheridan.
Carlyle, *Past and Present* and *French Revolution.*
Goethe, *Faust* and *Wilhelm Meister.*
Marivaux, *La Vie de Marianne.*

MODERN FICTION.

Selections from—Thackeray, Dickens, George Eliot,
    Kingsley, Scott, Bulwer-Lytton.

It must be borne in mind by the reader
that this list, although the one sent round
for criticism by the editor of the *Pall Mall
Gazette,* is not really Sir John Lubbock's.
This will be found on p. 240. Sir John
Lubbock's address was not given in full,
and the list drawn up by the *Pall Mall,*
from the reports in the daily papers, contained in fact only about 85 books.

It seems necessary to allude particularly
to this imperfect list, because it is the only
one upon which the critics were asked to
give an opinion, and their criticisms are
peculiarly interesting, as they give us an
important insight into the tastes and
opinions of our teachers. In itself it is
almost impossible to make a list that will

be practically useful, because tastes and needs differ so widely, that a course of reading suitable for one man may be quite unsuitable for another. It is also very doubtful whether a conscientious passage through a "cut-and-dried" list of books will feed the mind as a more original selection by each reader himself would do. It is probably best to start the student well on his way and then leave him to pursue it according to his own tastes. Each book will help him to another, and consultation with some of the many manuals of English literature will guide him towards a good choice. This is in effect what Mr. Bond, Principal Librarian of the British Museum, says in his reply to the circular of the editor of the *Pall Mall Gazette*. He writes —"The result of several persons putting down the titles of books they considered 'best reading' would be an interesting but very imperfect bibliography of as many sections of literature;" and, again, "The beginner should be advised to read histories of the literature of his own and other countries—as Hallam's 'Introduction to the Literature of Europe,' Joseph Warton's 'History of English Poetry,' Craik's 'History of English Literature,' Paine's History, and others of the same class. These would give him a survey of the field, and would quicken his taste for what was naturally most congenial to him."

There probably is no better course of reading than that which will naturally occur to one who makes an honest attempt to master our own noble literature. This is sufficient for the lifetime of most men without incursions into foreign literature. All cultivated persons will wish to become acquainted with the masterpieces of other nations, but this diversion will not be advisable if it takes the reader away from the study of the masterpieces of his own literature.

Turning to the comments on the *Pall Mall Gazette's* list, we may note one or two of the most important criticisms. The Prince of Wales very justly suggested that Dryden should not be omitted from such a list. Mr. Chamberlain asked whether the Bible was excluded by accident or design, and Mr. Irving suggested that the Bible and Shakespeare form together a very comprehensive library.

Mr. Ruskin's reply is particularly interesting, for he adds but little, contenting himself with the work of destruction. He writes, " Putting my pen lightly through the needless—and blottesquely through the rubbish and poison of Sir John's list—I leave enough for a life's liberal reading—and choice for any true worker's loyal reading. I have added one quite vital and essential book— Livy (the two first books), and three plays of Aristophanes (*Clouds*, *Birds*, and *Plutus*). Of travels, I read myself all old ones I can get hold of; of modern, Humboldt is the central model. Forbes (James Forbes in Alps) is essential to the modern Swiss tourist—of sense." Mr. Ruskin puts the word *all* to Plato, *everything* to Carlyle, and *every word* to Scott. Pindar's name he adds in the list of the classics, and after Bacon's name he writes " chiefly the *New Atlantis*."

The work of destruction is marked by the striking out of all the *Non-Christian Moralists*, of all the Theology and Devotion, with the exception of Jeremy Taylor and the *Pilgrim's Progress.* The Nibelungenlied and Malory's *Morte d'Arthur* (which, by the way, is in prose) go out, as do Sophocles and Euripides among the Greek Dramatists. *The Knights* is struck out to make way for the three plays of Aristophanes mentioned above. Gibbon, Voltaire, Hume, and Grote all go, as do all the philosophers but Bacon. Cook's Voyages and Darwin's Naturalist in the *Beagle* share a similar fate. Southey, Longfellow, Swift, Hume, Macaulay, and Emerson, Goethe and Marivaux, all are so unfortunate as to have Mr. Ruskin's pen driven through their names. Among the novelists Dickens and Scott only are left. The names of Thackeray, George Eliot, Kingsley, and Bulwer-Lytton are all erased.

Mr. Ruskin sent a second letter full of wisdom till he came to his reasons for striking out Grote's "History of Greece," "Confessions of St. Augustine," John Stuart

Mill, Charles Kingsley, Darwin, Gibbon, and Voltaire. With these reasons it is to be hoped that few readers will agree.

Mr. Swinburne makes a new list of his own which is very characteristic. No. 3 consists of " Selections from the Bible : comprising Job, the Psalms, Ecclesiastes, the Song of Solomon, Isaiah, Ezekiel, Joel ; the Gospels of St. Matthew and St. Luke, the Gospel and the First Epistle of St. John and Epistle of St. James." No. 12 is Villon, and Nos. 45 to 49 consist of the plays of Ford, Dekker, Tourneur, Marston, and Middleton ; names very dear to the lover of our old Drama, but I venture to think names somewhat inappropriate in a list of books for a reader who does not make the drama a speciality. Lamb's Selections would be sufficient for most readers.

Mr. William Morris supplies a full list with explanations, which are of considerable interest as coming from that distinguished poet.

Archdeacon Farrar gives, perhaps, the best test for a favourite author, that is, the selection of his works in the event of all others being destroyed. He writes, "But if all the books in the world were in a blaze, the first twelve which I should snatch out of the flames would be the Bible, *Imitatio Christi*, Homer, Æschylus, Thucydides, Tacitus, Virgil, Marcus Aurelius, Dante, Shakespeare, Milton, Wordsworth. Of living authors I would save first the works of Tennyson, Browning and Ruskin."

Another excellent test is that set up by travellers and soldiers. A book must be good when one of either of these classes decides to place it among his restricted baggage. Mr. H. M. Stanley writes, "You ask me what books I carried with me to take across Africa. I carried a great many— three loads, or about 180 lbs. weight; but as my men lessened in numbers, stricken by famine, fighting and sickness, they were one by one reluctantly thrown away, until finally, when less than 300 miles from the Atlantic, I possessed only the Bible, Shakespeare, Carlyle's Sartor Resartus, Norie's Navigation, and Nautical Almanac for 1877.

Poor Shakspeare was afterwards burned by demand of the foolish people of Zinga. At Bonea, Carlyle and Norie and Nautical Almanac were pitched away, and I had only the old Bible left." He then proceeds to give a list of books which he allowed himself when " setting out with a tidy battalion of men."

Lord Wolseley writes, "During the mutiny and China war I carried a Testament, two volumes of Shakespeare that contained his best plays, and since then, when in the field, I have always carried : Book of Common Prayer, Thomas à Kempis, Soldier's Pocket Book . . . . The book that I like reading at odd moments is 'The Meditations of Marcus Aurelius.' " He then adds, for any distant expedition, a few books of History (Creasy's " Decisive Battles," Plutarch's " Lives," Voltaire's " Charles XII.," " Cæsar," by Froude, and Hume's " England "). His Fiction is confined to Macaulay's " History of England " and the " Essays."

Mr. Quaritch remarks that " Sir John's 'working man' is an ideal creature. I have known many working men, but none of them could have suggested such a feast as he has prepared for them." He adds, "In my younger days I had no books whatever beyond my school books. Arrived in London in 1842, I joined a literary institution, and read all their historical works. To read fiction I had no time. A friend of mine read novels all night long, and was one morning found dead in his bed." If Mr. Quaritch intends this as a warning, he should present the fact for the consideration of those readers who swell the numbers of novels in the statistics of the Free Libraries.

Looking at the *Pall Mall Gazette's* list, it naturally occurs to us that it would be a great error for an Englishman to arrange his reading so that he excluded Chaucer while he included Confucius. Among the names of modern novelists it is strange that Jane Austen and Charlotte Brontë should have been omitted. In Sir John Lubbock's own list it will be seen that the names of Chaucer and Miss Austen occur. Among Essayists one would like to have seen at least the names

of Charles Lamb, De Quincey, and Landor,
and many will regret to find such delightful
writers as Walton and Thomas Fuller omitted.
We ought, however, to be grateful to Sir
John Lubbock for raising a valuable discussion which is likely to draw the attention
of many readers to books which might
otherwise have been most unjustly neglected
by them.[1]

The following is Sir John Lubbock's list.
It will be seen that several of the books,
whose absence is remarked on, do really
form part of the list, and that the objections
of the critics are so far met.

The Bible.

Marcus Aurelius, *Meditations.*
Epictetus.
Confucius, *Analects.*
Le Bouddha et sa Religion (St.-Hilaire).
Aristotle, *Ethics.*

----

[1] The whole of the correspondence has been re-
issued as a *Pall Mall "Extra,"* No. 24, and three-
pence will be well laid out by the purchaser of this
very interesting pamphlet.

Mahomet, *Koran* (parts of).

Apostolic Fathers, Wake's collection.
St. Augustine, *Confessions.*
Thomas à Kempis, *Imitation.*
Pascal, *Pensées.*
Spinoza, *Tractatus Theologico-Politicus.*
Comte, *Cat. of Positive Philosophy* (Congreve).
Butler, *Analogy.*
Jeremy Taylor, *Holy Living and Holy Dying.*
Bunyan, *Pilgrim's Progress.*
Keble, *Christian Year.*

Aristotle, *Politics.*
Plato's Dialogues—at any rate the *Phædo* and *Republic.*
Demosthenes, *De Coronâ.*
Lucretius.
Plutarch.
Horace.
Cicero, *De Officiis, De Amicitiâ, De Senectute.*

Homer, *Iliad* and *Odyssey.*
Hesiod.
Virgil.
Niebelungenlied.
Malory, *Morte d'Arthur.*

Maha-Bharata, Ramayana, epitomized by Talboys
    Wheeler in the first two vols. of his *History of India.*

16

Firdusi, *Shah-nameh.*   Translated by Atkinson.
She-king (Chinese Odes).

————

Æschylus, *Prometheus, House of Atreus,* Trilogy, or
    Persæ.
Sophocles, *Œdipus,* Trilogy.
Euripides, *Medea.*
Aristophanes, *The Knights.*

————

Herodotus.
Xenophon, *Anabasis.*
Thucydides.
Tacitus, *Germania.*
Livy.
Gibbon, *Decline and Fall.*
Hume, *England.*
Grote, *Greece.*
Carlyle, *French Revolution.*
Green, *Short History of England.*
Bacon, *Novum Organum.*
Mill, *Logic* and *Political Economy.*
Darwin, *Origin of Species.*
Smith, *Wealth of Nations* (part of).
Berkeley, *Human Knowledge.*
Descartes, *Discours sur la Méthode.*
Locke, *Conduct of the Understanding.*
Lewes, *History of Philosophy.*

————

Cook, *Voyages.*

Humboldt, *Travels.*
Darwin, *Naturalist in the Beagle.*

Shakespeare.
Milton, *Paradise Lost,* and the shorter poems.
Dante, *Divina Commedia.*
Spenser, *Faerie Queen.*
Dryden's Poems.
Chaucer, Morris's (or, if expurgated, Clarke's or Mrs.
    Haweis's) edition.
Gray.
Burns.
Scott's Poems.
Wordsworth, Mr. Arnold's selection.
Heine.
Pope.
Southey.

Goldsmith, *Vicar of Wakefield.*
Swift, *Gulliver's Travels.*
Defoe, *Robinson Crusoe.*
The Arabian Nights.
Cervantes, *Don Quixote.*
Boswell, *Johnson.*
Burke, *Select Works* (Payne).
Essayists : — Bacon, Addison, Hume, Montaigne,
    Macaulay, Emerson.
Molière.
Sheridan.

Voltaire, *Zadig.*
Carlyle, *Past and Present.*
Goethe, *Faust, Wilhelm Meister.*
White, *Natural History of Selborne.*
Smiles, *Self Help.*

———

Miss Austen, either *Emma* or *Pride and Prejudice.*
Thackeray, *Vanity Fair* and *Pendennis.*
Dickens, *Pickwick* and *David Copperfield.*
George Eliot, *Adam Bede.*
Kingsley, *Westward Ho!*
Bulwer-Lytton, *Last Days of Pompeii.*
Scott's Novels.

INDEX.

For EU product safety concerns, contact us at Calle de José Abascal, 56–1°,
28003 Madrid, Spain or eugpsr@cambridge.org.

www.ingramcontent.com/pod-product-compliance
Ingram Content Group UK Ltd.
Pitfield, Milton Keynes, MK11 3LW, UK
UKHW010342140625
459647UK00010B/759